INTERMEDIATE GERMAN:
A GRAMMAR AND WORKBOOK

Intermediate German is designed for learners who have achieved basic proficiency and wish to progress to more complex language. Its 24 units present a broad range of grammatical topics, illustrated by examples which serve as models for varied exercises that follow. These exercises enable the student to master the relevant grammar points.

Features include:

- authentic German, from a range of media, used throughout the book to reflect German culture, life and society

- illustrations of grammar points in English as well as German

- checklists at the end of each unit for consolidation

- cross-referencing to other grammar units in the book

- glossary of grammatical terminology

- full answer key to all exercises

Suitable for independent learners and students on taught courses, *Intermediate German*, together with its sister volume, *Basic German*, forms a structured course in the essentials of German.

Anna Miell is University Lecturer in German at the University of Westminster and at Trinity College of Music in Greenwich and works as a language consultant in London. **Heiner Schenke** is Senior Lecturer of German at the University of Westminster and has published a number of language books.

Other titles available in the *Grammar Workbook* series are:

Basic Cantonese
Intermediate Cantonese

Basic German

Basic Italian

Basic Polish
Intermediate Polish

Basic Russian
Intermediate Russian

Basic Spanish

Basic Welsh
Intermediate Welsh

Titles of related interest published by Routledge:

Colloquial German
by Dietlinde Hatherall and Glyn Hatherall

Modern German Grammar: A Practical Guide, Second Edition
by William Dodd, Christine Eckhard-Black, John Klapper
and Ruth Whittle

Modern German Grammar Workbook, Second Edition
by William Dodd, Christine Eckhard-Black, John Klapper
and Ruth Whittle

INTERMEDIATE GERMAN: A GRAMMAR AND WORKBOOK

Anna Miell and Heiner Schenke

Routledge
Taylor & Francis Group

LONDON AND NEW YORK

First published 2006
by Routledge
2 Park Square, Milton Park, Abingdon, Oxon OX14 4RN

Simultaneously published in the USA and Canada
by Routledge
270 Madison Ave, New York, NY 10016

Routledge is an imprint of the Taylor & Francis Group, an informa business

© 2006 Anna Miell and Heiner Schenke

Typeset in Times Ten and Helvetica by
Florence Production Ltd, Stoodleigh, Devon
Printed and bound in Great Britain by
TJ International Ltd, Padstow, Cornwall

British Library Cataloguing in Publication Data
A catalogue record for this book is available from the
British Library

Library of Congress Cataloging in Publication Data
Miell, Anna.
  Intermediate German: a grammar and workbook / by
  Anna Miell & Heiner Schenke
      p. cm. – (Grammar workbook series)
    1. German language – Grammar.   2. German language
– Textbooks for foreign speakers – English.   I. Schenke,
Heiner.   II. Title.   III. Routledge grammars.   IV. Series.
  PF3112.M44 2006
  438.2'421 – dc 22   2006005339

ISBN10: 0–415–28406–6 (hbk)
ISBN10: 0–415–28407–4 (pbk)
ISBN10: 0–203–32557–5 (ebk)

ISBN13: 978–0–415–28406–6 (hbk)
ISBN13: 978–0–415–28407–3 (pbk)
ISBN13: 978–0–203–32557–5 (ebk)

CONTENTS

PREFACE

Intermediate German is aimed at learners of German who have acquired the basics of the language and want to progress further. It is also ideal for intermediate to advanced learners who want to consolidate and extend their knowledge of German grammar. The book can be used on its own or in connection with any major German coursebook and is suitable for self-study, class-based learning or reference purposes.

Presentation of grammar

The book explains the essentials of German grammar in clear and simple language. The format is easily accessible and grammar topics follow a progression, which move from simple aspects to more complex features. For more in-depth study, there are cross-references to related grammar items. Explanations are simple and avoid specialised terminology whenever possible while introducing key terms. The vocabulary is practical and functional.

Structure of units

There are 24 units. Each unit covers one key grammar topic, which is contrasted with English structures where appropriate. Most topic starts out with an overview. This is usually followed by detailed explanation in an easy to follow step-by-step layout, breaking down complex aspects into simple segments. Examples in English and German illustrate each point and introduce relevant vocabulary.

Checklists and exercises

Integrated exercises allow immediate transfer and practice to consolidate each grammar point. Exercises are varied and progress from simple recognition to more complex application of grammar points.

A checklist at the end of each unit reinforces main points and provides an opportunity to self-assess understanding of the material covered.

Answers to all exercises and the checklists are available in a key at the end of the book.

Using the book as a grammar reference

Unit headings indicate which grammar point is covered and the index at the end of the book refers users to the relevant units. The glossary provides clear definitions and simple explanations of key grammatical terms. When appropriate, cross-references are provided within units.

Extra features

Extra tips on how to make language learning easier and more successful are provided wherever appropriate. The book also gives the learner up-to-date information on the contemporary usage of grammatical structures in German.

The book is suitable for:

- lower intermediate to advanced students
- AS/A-level revision
- courses at university and in further education
- adult education courses
- independent learners.

UNIT ONE
Nouns and gender

What are nouns?

Nouns are words used to name living creatures, objects, abstract qualities or concepts:

Mann	man	**Rock**	skirt
Schönheit	beauty	**Entwicklung**	development

German nouns – three genders

In German, all nouns are classed as having one of three genders: *masculine*, *feminine* or *neuter* and are written with an initial capital letter. In dictionaries, the gender is usually indicated with *m* for masculine nouns, *f* for feminine nouns and *nt* for neuter nouns.

Working out the gender

Often there seems to be no obvious relationship between a noun and its gender in German: **Rock** 'skirt' for instance is masculine, **Hose** 'trousers' is feminine and **Kleid** 'dress' is neuter.

However, there are two main ways that can help you to work out the gender:

- certain endings indicate the gender
- some groups of nouns, usually linked by meaning, tend to be masculine or feminine or neuter.

Endings indicating the gender

Masculine endings

The following endings usually indicate that the noun is masculine:

-ant	der Konsonant	consonant
-ast	der Palast	palace
-ich	der Teppich	carpet
-ig	der Honig	honey
-ling	der Liebling	darling
-or	der Motor	engine
-us	der Materialismus	materialism

An exception is **das Labor** 'laboratory'.

Feminine endings

The following endings tend to belong to feminine nouns:

-a	die Pizza	pizza
-anz	die Toleranz	tolerance
-ei	die Wäscherei	laundry
-enz	die Intelligenz	intelligence
-heit	die Mehrheit	majority
-ie	die Astrologie	astrology
-ik	die Musik	music
-ion	die Kommunikation	communication
-keit	die Müdigkeit	tiredness
-tät	die Kreativität	creativity
-schaft	die Erbschaft	inheritance
-ung	die Bedeutung	meaning, importance
-ur	die Frisur	hairstyle

Some exceptions are: **das Sofa** 'sofa', **das Genie** 'genius', **das Abitur** 'A levels'.

Note that about 90 per cent of nouns ending in **-e** are also feminine:

die Anzeige	advert	**die Karriere**	career
die Frage	question	**die Schokolade**	chocolate

Exceptions include: **das Auge** 'eye', **das Interesse** 'interest', **der Käse** 'cheese', **der Name** 'name', and all male persons and animals endings in **-e**: **der Junge** 'boy', **der Löwe** 'lion' etc.

Neuter endings

The following endings signal that a noun is neuter:

-chen	**das Märchen**	fairy tale
-il	**das Ventil**	valve
-lein	**das Männlein**	little man
-ma	**das Drama**	drama
-ment	**das Instrument**	instrument
-o	**das Auto**	car
-um	**das Zentrum**	centre

Some exceptions are: **die Firma** 'company', **der Reichtum** 'wealth'.

Groups of nouns

There are also certain groups of nouns, usually linked by meaning, which tend to be *masculine* or *feminine* or *neuter*:

Masculine	Feminine	Neuter
Male persons and male animals:	*Female persons and female animals*:	*Young persons and young animals*:
der Journalist, der Tiger	**die Journalistin, die Katze**	**das Kind, das Küken**
Days, months and seasons:	*Motorbikes and ships*:	*Most countries, towns*:
der Montag, der August, der Sommer	**die BMW, die Titanic**	**Deutschland, Berlin** (usually used without article)
Makes of cars:	*Numerals*:	*Hotels, cafés, cinemas*:
der BMW, der Toyota	**die Eins, die Million**	**das Hilton, das Café Flore**
Alcoholic drinks:	*Names of trees and flowers*:	*Metals and chemicals*:
der Wein, der Schnaps	**die Eiche, die Orchidee**	**das Silber, das Helium**
Many other drinks:	*Names of most native rivers*:	*Infinitives used as nouns*:
der Kaffee, der Saft	**die Donau, die Elbe**	**das Singen, das Tanzen**
Points of the compass:		*Foreign words ending in*
der Norden, der Westen		**-ing: das Meeting, das Training**

Masculine	Feminine	Neuter
Most currencies: **der Euro, der Dollar**		*Diminutives*: **das Händchen** ('little hand') **das Tischlein** ('little table')
Exceptions include: **das Bier, das Wasser**; **das Britische Pfund** (Sterling)	*Exceptions include:* **das Mädchen** and the following rivers: **der Main, der Rhein, der Neckar**	*Exceptions include:* **der Irak, die Schweiz, die Türkei, die Ukraine, die Niederlande** (plural), **die USA** (plural)

Compound nouns

The last noun defines the gender

Compound nouns usually consist of two or more nouns. The gender is defined by the last noun:

> **der Computer + das Spiel → das Computerspiel**
> computer game

> **der Bauch + der Tanz + die Lehrerin → die Bauchtanzlehrerin**
> teacher of belly dancing

Adding -s

When joining *noun + noun* together an extra **-s** is often inserted to link the components and to make the pronunciation easier. This usually happens when the first noun ends in **-heit, -ing, -ion, -keit, -ling, -schaft, -tät** or **-ung**:

> **der Liebling + die Band** → **die Lieblingsband**
> favourite band

> **die Mehrheit + der Beschluss** → **der Mehrheitsbeschluss**
> majority decision

Nouns in use

Determiners and nouns

When used in sentences, nouns normally appear with determiners such as **der**, **die**, **das** etc. Depending on the function of the noun within the sentence the determiners can change.

For example, the definite articles **der**, **die**, **das** and **die** for plural nouns are used when the noun is the subject of a sentence (*nominative case*). These articles change to **dem**, **der**, **dem**, **den** if the noun is the indirect object (*dative case*).

Changes affecting nouns

Note that nouns themselves normally change only (other than their plural forms) in the following instances:

- in the *genitive case*, where masculine and neuter nouns add **-(e)s** and
- in the *dative plural* where **-n** is usually added.

For more information see Units 3 and 4.

However, there are two groups of nouns whose endings do change: the so-called *weak nouns* and *adjectival nouns*.

Weak nouns

About 10 per cent of masculine nouns, usually referring to male people or animals, add **-(e)n** to all forms apart from the *nominative singular*.

	Singular	*Plural*
Nominative	**der Junge**	**die Junge-n**
Accusative	**den Junge-n**	**die Junge-n**
Dative	**dem Junge-n**	**den Junge-n**
Genitive	**des Junge-n**	**der Junge-n**

Der Junge spielt mit seinem Gameboy.	(*nom., sing.*)
Siehst du den Jungen dort?	(*acc., sing.*)
Er kauft dem Jungen eine Flasche Wasser.	(*dat., sing.*)

Other examples include: **Architekt** 'male architect', **Student** 'male student', **Herr** 'Mr', 'gentleman', **Tourist** 'male tourist', **Mensch** 'human being', **Name** 'name'.

Note that **Herr** adds **-n** in the singular, and **-en** in the plural: **Kennst du Herrn Becker** 'Do you know Mr Becker?' **Meine Damen und Herren!** 'Ladies and gentlemen!'.

Adjectival nouns

Adjectival nouns are derived from adjectives:

krank	→ **ein Kranker, eine Kranke**	ill, sick person
reich	**ein Reicher, eine Reiche**	rich person
verwandt	**ein Verwandter, eine Verwandte**	relative

Adjectives used as nouns follow the pattern of adjectival endings. As an example, here are all forms of **Verwandte/r** 'relative' with the indefinite article:

	Singular (masc.)	*Singular (fem.)*	*Plural*
Nominative	**ein Verwandter**	**eine Verwandte**	**-Verwandte**
Accusative	**einen Verwandten**	**eine Verwandte**	**-Verwandte**
Dative	**einem Verwandten**	**einer Verwandten**	**-Verwandten**
Genitive	**eines Verwandten**	**einer Verwandten**	**-Verwandter**

Ein Verwandter von mir wohnt in Bonn. (*nom., masc.*)
One of my relatives lives in Bonn.

Eine Verwandte von Petra arbeitet bei Sony. (*nom., fem.*)
One of Petra's relatives works for Sony.

Other nouns belonging to this group include:

Angestellte/r	employee	**Arbeitslose/r**	unemployed person
Erwachsene/r	adult	**Deutsche/r**	German person
Jugendliche/r	young person		

- For the plural forms of nouns, see Unit 2.
- For more detailed information on determiners and cases, see Units 3 and 4.
- For more details on adjectival endings, see Unit 15.

Exercise 1.1

Here is a list of nouns with different endings. Can you identify their gender and enter the nouns with the definite article in the table below? The first one has been done for you.

> Frühling, König, Universität, Exil, Mädchen, Fabrik,
> Pfennig, Tischlein, Ewigkeit, Museum, Freiheit, Religion, Reise,
> Humanismus, Video, Schwächling, Motor, Thema, Zyklus,
> Tortur, Rechnung, Element, Eleganz, Honig, Diamant, Büro,
> Bedeutung, Instrument, Konsonant, Auto.

Masculine	Feminine	Neuter
der Frühling *der Honig* *die Bedeutung die Freiheit* *das Auto der Tischlein*		

[handwritten answers filling the table:]

Masculine: der Frühling, der Honig, der Schwächling, der Konsonant, der Diamant, der Motor, der Zyklus, der Pfennig

Feminine: die Bedeutung, die Freiheit, die Rechnung, die Uni, die Ewigkeit, die Mädchen, die Eleganz, die Thema, die Religion, die Tortur, die Reise, die Fabrik

Neuter: das Auto, das Tischlein, das Exil, das Element, das Büro, das Instrument, das Video, das Museum

[margin note: der Humanismus]

Exercise 1.2

Now write out the endings from Exercise 1.1. that are typical for masculine, feminine and neuter nouns.

M *ant, ast, ich, ig, ling, or, us*
F *a, anz, ei, enz, heit, ie, ik, ion, keit, tät, schaft, ung, ur*
N *chen, lein, um, ma, ment, o, um*

Exercise 1.3

Each of the following lines contains one noun that does not share its gender with those next to it. Indicate the odd one out and note the gender for all other nouns at the beginning of each line:

Example:

_____ **Wein, Jaguar, April, Bier, Samstag, Euro, Norden** →
masculine **Wein, Jaguar, April, *Bier*, Samstag, Euro, Norden**

1 *fem* Frau, Billion, Themse, Katze, Ingenieurin, Rhein
2 *masc* Iran, Labor, Motor, Rhein, Winter, Pfennig, Nissan
3 *neut* Essen, Baby, Silber, Ritz, Marketing, Schweiz, Lamm
4 *fem* Katze, Milliarde, Tochter, Mädchen, Harley-Davidson
5 *masc* Sommer, Wasser, Dienstag, Tee, September, Dollar

Exercise 1.4

Translate the following sentences into German.

1   The Mercedes is very fast.
2   What does the car cost?
3   The newspaper costs 1 Euro.
4   Here is the mother but where is the girl?
5   When does the meeting begin?
6   Here is the tea without milk.
7   The water comes from France.
8   The computer game was interesting.
9   Do you know Mr Schmidt? (*Use the **Sie** form.*)
10   Ladies and gentlemen!

Checklist	✓
1 What are the two main ways that can help you recognise the gender of nouns?	
2 Can you name at least four typical masculine endings, four neuter ones and six feminine ones?	
3 What is a compound noun and how do you spot its gender?	
4 Do you know what makes weak nouns different from other masculine nouns?	

UNIT TWO
Plural of nouns

Plural forms in German

In English most nouns form their plural by adding '-s' to the singular form. In German, there are several ways of forming the plural.

However, there are patterns and clues that might help you to predict the plural endings:

- there are five main types of plural endings (listed below)
- nouns tend to take certain endings according to their gender.

The five main plural forms – overview

Here is an overview of the five main and three related types of plural endings in German:

1 *-e*	2 *-er*	3 *-(e)n*	4 *-*	5 *-s*
der Tag	das Bild	die Frau	der Wagen	der Park
die Tag-e	die Bild-er	die Frau-en	die Wagen	die Park-s

umlaut + -e	*umlaut + -er*		*umlaut*	
die Hand	der Wald		die Mutter	
die Händ-e	die Wäld-er		die Mütter	

Plural endings for masculine nouns

Most take -e or ⁻e endings

Most masculine nouns take **-e** or **⁻e** in their plural forms:

-e *or*	→	**der Arm**	– **die Arme**	**der Schuh**	– **die Schuhe**
⁻e		**der Ball**	– **die Bälle**	**der Fuß**	– **die Füße**

In addition, there are two more main plural endings for masculine nouns:

no ending	→	**der Onkel**	– **die Onkel**	**der Spiegel**	– **die Spiegel**
or					
+ *umlaut*		**der Apfel**	– **die Äpfel**	**der Vater**	– **die Väter**

-(e)n   →   This ending applies to so-called *weak nouns* usually referring to male people or animals:

der Junge → **die Jungen**   **der Elefant** → **die Elefanten**

Other endings

A few masculine nouns add **-er** and an **umlaut** wherever possible. They include:

der Mann → **die Männer**   **der Wald** → **die Wälder**

Plural endings for feminine nouns

Most take -(e)n

Most feminine nouns take the plural ending **-(e)n**. This applies to all nouns ending in **-e**, **-ei**, **-heit**, **-ion**, **-keit**, **-schaft**, **-tät**, **-ung** or **-ur**:

-(e)n	→	**die Blume**	– **die Blumen**
		die Bäckerei	– **die Bäckereien**
		die Tasche	– **die Taschen**
		die Zeitung	– **die Zeitungen**

In addition, there are two more commonly used endings with feminine nouns:

-e +   →   This ending applies to many feminine nouns consisting
umlaut   of one syllable:

die Frucht	–	die Früchte	die Hand	–	die Hände
die Nacht	–	die Nächte	die Stadt	–	die Städte

-nen   →   Female nouns with the ending **-in** add **-nen**:

die Freundin → **die Freundinnen**

Other endings

A few feminine nouns only add an umlaut to their plural forms. The most important are: **die Mutter** → **die Mütter** and **die Tochter** → **die Töchter**.

Plural endings for neuter nouns

Most take **-e**

Here are the three main plural endings for neuter nouns:

-e   →   This ending is the most common with neuter nouns:

das Bein	–	die Beine	das Jahr	–	die Jahre
das Regal	–	die Regale	das Stück	–	die Stücke

-er *or*   → | das Kind | – | die Kinder | das Kleid | – | die Kleider |
¨er *(when* | das Gehalt– | die Gehälter | das Glas | – | die Gläser |
possible)

no change →   There is no change for most neuter nouns ending in **-el**, **-er**, **chen** and **-lein**:

das Segel	–	die Segel	das Mädchen	–	die Mädchen
das Messer –	die Messer	das Männlein –	die Männlein

Other endings

A few neuter nouns have **-(e)n** in the plural. They include: **das Auge** → **die Augen, das Bett** → **die Betten, das Interesse** → **die Interessen**.

Plural endings with -s

All three genders have some plural endings with **-s**. However, this type of ending is mainly used for words imported from foreign languages, in abbreviations and names:

das Hotel	→	die Hotels
der PC	→	die PCs
Herr und Frau Schmidt	→	die Schmidts

Foreign nouns which don't add an -s in the plural include: **der Manager → die Manager, der Computer → die Computer**.

Also note that words from the English which end in '-y' have the German plural form **-ys**: **die Party → die Partys**.

Points to watch out for

Nouns from Greek and Latin

A number of words imported from Greek or Latin have the following plural patterns:

- nouns ending in **-us** or **-um** change its ending to **-en** in the plural:

    der Organismus → die Organismen
    das Museum → die Museen

- most nouns which end in **-ma** replace this form with **-men**:

    die Firma → die Firmen
    das Thema → die Themen

Plural endings in the dative

Plurals in the dative case normally add the letter **-n** wherever this is possible.

Die Bäume sind grün.	→	**Sie liegen unter den Bäumen.**
(*nom. pl.*)		(*dat. pl.*)
The trees are green.		They lie under the trees.

The plural endings in **-s** stay the same: **Mit so vielen Autos hatte niemand gerechnet** 'Nobody had reckoned with that many cars'.

Nouns used in the plural only

Note that some German nouns are used only in their plural form. They include: **Eltern** 'parents', **Ferien** 'holidays', **Geschwister** 'brother(s) and sister(s)', **Lebensmittel** 'food', **Leute** 'people', **Möbel** 'furniture'.

Looking up plural forms

Note that dictionaries also give information on plural nouns. You can usually find the plural ending or form of a noun after its gender and genitive case ending:

Vater *m* -s, ¨ father   →   **die Väter**
Baby *nt* -s, -s baby   **die Babys**
Telefon *nt* -s, -e telephone   **die Telefone**

- For more detail on gender of nouns, see Unit 1.

Exercise 2.1

Here are five groups of nouns in the singular. Look at the plural endings in the box and match them to each column. The first one has been done for you.

¨e	¨er	-e	-(e)n	–

1 ¨e	2 ‑ en	3 ‑	4 e	5 er
Ball e	Blume n	Wagen	Tag e	Wald er
Fuß o	Frau en	Onkel	Arm e	Mann er
Hand e	Bäckerei en	Mädchen	Beruf e	Dorf er
Ton e	Tasche n	Messer	Schuh e	Glas er

Exercise 2.2

Give the plural of the following nouns.

Example: **der Mann → die *Männer***

1 der Beruf   die _Berufe_
2 der Fuß   die _Füße_
3 der Spiegel   die _Spiegel_
4 die Stadt   die _Städte_ ×
5 die Kultur   die _Kulturen_
6 die Friseurin   die _Friseurinnen_
11 das Radio   die _Radios_
12 das Hotel   die _Hotels_
13 der PC   die _PCs_
14 der Manager   die _Manager_
15 das Zentrum   die _Zentren_
16 das Thema   die _Themen_

7 das Gehalt   die _____   17 der Park   die _____
8 das Telefon   die _____   18 die Firma   die _____
9 das Bild   die _____   19 das Regal   die _____
10 das Jahr   die _____   20 der Wald   die _____

Exercise 2.3

Translate the sentences below into German.

1 I work three days per week.
2 He likes flowers.
3 The parties are on Friday and Saturday.
4 The two companies are in Frankfurt.
5 The people come from Paris.
6 We visit the churches and then the museums.
7 The hotels are modern.
8 We need two computers.
9 The children read together.
10 She plays with the children.

Checklist	✓
1 Do you know the most common plural endings for masculine nouns?	
2 How do nearly all feminine nouns form their plural?	
3 How do most foreign words in German form their plural?	
4 Can you list the five main forms of plural endings?	
5 What is special about plural endings in the dative?	

UNIT THREE
Articles and other determiners

The two articles and other determiners

Determiners usually precede nouns. The most important ones are the *definite article*, such as **der**, **die** etc. corresponding to 'the', and the *indefinite article*, such as **ein**, **eine** etc. corresponding to 'a'.

Other determiners include:

- *possessives* such as **mein** 'my', **dein** 'your', etc.
- *demonstratives* such as **dieser** 'this'
- *indefinites* such as **alle** 'all'/'everybody'.

Importance of determiners in German

Determiners signal various aspects of the noun

Determiners play an important role in German as they indicate whether a noun is *masculine, feminine* or *neuter* and if the noun is in the *singular* or *plural* form. Furthermore, determiners signal the *grammatical function* of a noun in a sentence (if it is the *subject, direct object* etc.).

How determiners can change

Look at the following examples with the *definite article*:

Der Manager hat in Washington studiert.
(*masc., sing., subject = nominative*)

Kennst du den Manager?
(*masc., sing., direct object = accusative*)

Was gibt er dem Manager?
(*masc., sing., indirect object = dative*)

As you can see, the definite article changes in accordance with the gender, number and case of the noun it is linked to. This process is called *declension*.

In the following sections the main determiners and their declension pattern are shown in more detail.

The definite article

Referring to a specific noun

The definite article is used before a noun when referring to a specific or somehow known person, thing or idea:

Die Hauptstadt von Deutschland ist Berlin.
The capital of Germany is Berlin.

Differences between German and English

The use of the definite article can sometimes differ in English and German. The definite article is used in German with:

- *names of countries* which have masculine or feminine gender such as **der Irak**, **die Schweiz**, and names of countries in the plural form (**die USA**);

- *institutions* such as schools and street names:

    Nadine geht in die Schule.
    Nadine goes to school.

    Er wohnt in der Goethestraße.
    He lives in Goethestrasse.

- *months* and *seasons* such as **der Sommer** '(the) summer', **der August** 'August' etc. and *meals*:

    Der August was schön.
    August was lovely.

    Nach dem Mittagessen ...
    After lunch ...

- *abstract nouns* such as **Leben** 'life', **Natur** 'nature', **Kunst** 'art' and often with *infinitives used as nouns*:

    Das Leben in London ist sehr teuer.
    Life in London is very expensive.

Ich fürchte mich vor dem Fliegen.
I am afraid of flying.

Declension

As explained above, the definite article changes its form according to gender, number and case of the noun it precedes. Here are all forms:

	Masculine		Feminine		Neuter		Plural	
Nom.	de**r**	**Mann**	di**e**	**Frau**	da**s**	**Kind**	di**e**	**Leute**
Acc.	de**n**	**Mann**	di**e**	**Frau**	da**s**	**Kind**	di**e**	**Leute**
Dat.	de**m**	**Mann**	de**r**	**Frau**	de**m**	**Kind**	de**n**	**Leute**n
Gen.	de**s**	**Mannes**	de**r**	**Frau**	de**s**	**Kindes**	de**r**	**Leute**

Merging of definite articles and prepositions

When using definite articles with prepositions such as **in**, **an, auf** the two words often merge: **Er ist *in dem* Garten.** → **Er ist *im* Garten.** 'He is in the garden'. For more information on shortened forms of the definite article, see Unit 16.

The indefinite article

Referring to an unspecified noun

An indefinite article before a noun refers to an unspecified person, thing or idea:

Kennst du ein Hotel in München?
Do you know a hotel in Munich?

Differences between German and English

The use of the indefinite article in English and German is very similar, although there are a few differences:

• There is no indefinite article in German when stating an affiliation to a country, city, profession or religion:

Ich bin Amerikaner.
I am an American.

Franz ist Berliner.
Franz is a Berliner.

Frau Gass ist Sozialarbeiterin.
Mrs Gass is a social worker.

- But the indefinite article is used when an adjective is placed before the noun:

Sie ist eine gebürtige Kölnerin.
She was born in Cologne.

Max ist ein sehr guter Webdesigner.
Max is a very good web designer.

- While some nouns function without any article it is important to remember that, put in the negative, the appropriate form of **kein** has to be used:

Er ist kein Katholik und sie ist keine gebürtige Londonerin.
He isn't a Catholic and she isn't a born Londoner.

Declension

Here are all the various forms of the indefinite article:

	Masculine		Feminine		Neuter		Plural
Nom.	ein	Beruf	eine	Adresse	ein	Telefon	– Bücher
Acc.	einen	Beruf	eine	Adresse	ein	Telefon	– Bücher
Dat.	einem	Beruf	einer	Adresse	einem	Telefon	– Büchern
Gen.	eines	Berufs	einer	Adresse	eines	Telefons	– Bücher

The possessives

Indicating ownership

The possessives **mein** 'my', **dein** 'your', **Ihr** 'your', **sein** 'his', **ihr** 'her', **sein** 'its', **unser** 'our', **euer** 'your' (*informal*), **Ihr** 'your' (*formal*), **ihr** 'their', refer to ownership or belonging and relate to the noun they precede:

Sind Sie mit Ihrem Beruf zufrieden?
Are you happy with your job?

Declension pattern

The possessives follow the declension pattern of the indefinite article. As an example, here are all forms of **Ihr** 'your' (*formal*):

	Masculine		*Feminine*		*Neuter*		*Plural*	
Nom.	**Ihr**	**Beruf**	**Ihr**e	**Adresse**	**Ihr**	**Telefon**	**Ihr**e	**Bücher**
Acc.	**Ihr**en	**Beruf**	**Ihr**e	**Adresse**	**Ihr**	**Telefon**	**Ihr**e	**Bücher**
Dat.	**Ihr**em	**Beruf**	**Ihr**er	**Adresse**	**Ihr**em	**Telefon**	**Ihr**en	**Büchern**
Gen.	**Ihr**es	**Beruf**s	**Ihr**er	**Adresse**	**Ihr**es	**Telefon**s	**Ihr**er	**Bücher**

Spelling variations for euer

Note that **euer** loses its second *e* in nearly all declension forms, except for the *masculine nominative*: **euer Ball** and *neuter nominative* and *accusative*: **euer Baby**.

Ist das euer Ball?
(*masculine nominative*)

Wir haben euren Ball gefunden.
(*masculine accusative*)

Demonstratives – dieser, solcher

Pointing out a specific noun

Demonstrative determiners single out specific people, objects, qualities, concepts etc. The most important determiner is **dieser** 'this'/'that' which refers to a noun in close proximity or previously mentioned:

Dieser Bus fährt in die Stadt.
This/that bus goes into town.

Kennst du diese Leute?
Do you know these people?

Another frequently used demonstrative is **solcher** 'such':

Solchen Unsinn habe ich schon lange nicht mehr gehört.
I haven't heard such nonsense in a long time.

Declension pattern

Demonstratives follow a very similar declension pattern as the definite article. Here are all the forms of **dieser**:

	Masculine	Feminine	Neuter	Plural
Nom.	dieser Mann	diese Frau	dieses Kind	diese Leute
Acc.	diesen Mann	diese Frau	dieses Kind	diese Leute
Dat.	diesem Mann	dieser Frau	diesem Kind	diesen Leuten
Gen.	dieses Mannes	dieser Frau	dieses Kindes	dieser Leute

Indefinites – jeder, einige, viel(e), alle

Referring to a group or to a part

Indefinites usually refer to parts of something or to a whole group, and not to a specific person or object. The most important indefinites are: **jeder** 'each'/'every', **einige** 'some'/'any', **viel(e)** 'much'/'many' and **alle** 'all'/'everybody':

Jedes Kind bekommt ein Eis.
Every child gets an ice cream.

Einige Leute konnten nicht kommen.
Some people couldn't come.

Viele Köche verderben den Brei.
Many cooks spoil the broth.

Allen Kompositionen von Mozart wurde eine Katalogsnummer gegeben.
All the compositions by Mozart were given a catalogue number.

Declension pattern

The indefinites follow the same declension pattern as **dieser**. Note that **einige** 'some'/'any' and **alle** 'all'/'everybody' can only be used in the plural.

viel(e) usually appears without ending before singular nouns and 'uncountable' nouns when used in the sense of 'much'/'a lot of':

Er trinkt viel Bier.
He drinks a lot of beer.

Sie hat viel Mut.
She has a lot of courage.

- For more detail on the functions and cases of nouns, see Unit 4.
- For the use of determiners as pronouns, see Unit 5.

Exercise 3.1

One of the two nouns in each of the following sentences is used with an article and one without any article. Indicate the noun without an article with an X and fill in the other gap with an article from the box below.

---

der das der dem der eine der

Example:
Ergün kommt aus _____ Türkei und spielt gern _____ Klavier. →
Ergün kommt aus *der* Türkei und spielt gern *X* Klavier.

1 Frau Bäcker ist _____ Bankkauffrau und wohnt in _der_
   Ottomannstraße.
2 Ich finde _das_ Leben als _X_ Journalist ziemlich gut.
3 Er ist _X_ Österreicher, aber sie ist _eine_ gebürtige Französin.
4 Karin ist in _dem_ Schweiz geboren und ist _X_ Ärztin.
5 Nach _____ Abendessen werden sie _____ Gitarre spielen.
6 In _der_ Schule lernen wir viel über _X_ Großbritannien.

Exercise 3.2

Fill in each gap below by supplying an appropriate possessive with the correct ending. Note that all sentences are in direct speech.

Example: **Connie, ist das _____ Buch?** →
          Connie, ist das *dein* Buch?

1 Wo hast du eigentlich _____ Schuhe gekauft?
2 Wann beginnt Sabine mit _____ Arbeit?
3 Frau Merz, vergessen Sie bloß nicht _____ Terminkalender!
4 Was schenkt Michael _____ Freundin zum Geburtstag?
5 Paul und Johannes, habt ihr _____ Joggingschuhe eingepackt?
6 Marlene und Lisa, habt ihr schon mit _____ Freunden telefoniert?

Exercise 3.3

Fill in the missing endings where appropriate.

1 Kennst du diesen Mann?
2 Fahren Sie mit diesem Auto?
3 Er hat solches Glück gehabt!
4 Einige Leute kamen zu spät.
5 Ich möchte alle Gäste willkommen heißen.
6 Er sprach mit allen Gästen.
7 Sie hat viele CDs zu Hause.
8 Trink nicht so viel Bier.

Exercise 3.4

Translate the following sentences into German.

1   After lunch we go for a walk.
2   They love life.
3   She is a Londoner.
4   Have you found your bag? (*Use the **du**, **Sie** and **ihr** forms.*)
5   I don't understand this question.
6   I have not seen this film.
7   He drinks a lot of coffee.
8   She's got many friends.
9   I haven't heard such nonsense in a long time.
10   All friends were there.

Checklist	✓
1 Can you name three determiners apart from the definite and indefinite articles?	
2 Do you know three instances where you would use a definite article in German but not in English?	
3 When would you use an indefinite article in English but not in German?	
4 What is the grammatical role of determiners in German?	

UNIT FOUR
Cases

What are cases?

A case refers to the role a noun or a pronoun plays in a particular sentence or clause. There are four main functions and each one can be linked to a specific case in German:

Case	Function of noun/pronoun	Example
Nom.	The noun/pronoun is the *subject* of the sentence, i.e. the 'agent' of what is happening.	**Der Schüler kauft einen Computer.** 'The pupil buys a computer'.
Acc.	It is the *direct object* of a sentence, i.e. the 'receiver' of the action.	**Die Lehrerin lobt den Schüler.** 'The teacher praises the pupil'.
Dat.	It is the **indirect object**, an additional object to whom/which the action is done.	**Er schenkt ihr eine DVD.** 'He gives her a DVD'.
Gen.	It indicates **possession** or ownership between two nouns.	**Das ist das Auto meines Bruders.** 'This is my brother's car'.

Changes caused by the case system

Changes to articles and determiners

The various functions and therefore the cases of nouns are usually signalled by the endings of articles and other determiners. When, for instance, a masculine noun is the *subject* in a sentence and in the *nominative,* the definite article would be **der**. If, however a masculine noun acts as the *direct object*, **der** must change to **den** as it is now in the *accusative*:

nom.   *Der* **Schüler kauft einen Computer.**
acc.   **Die Lehrerin lobt** *den* **Schüler.**

Different pronoun forms

Pronouns also have different forms. The personal pronoun **er** in the nominative changes to **ihn** in the accusative: *Er* **kauft einen Computer** 'He buys a computer'; **Die Lehrerin lobt** *ihn* 'The teacher praises him'.

Pronouns and cases will be explained in more detail in Unit 5.

Other factors that determine the use of cases

Note that apart from the function a noun performs in a sentence or clause, cases can also be 'triggered' by two other main factors:

- certain verbs which are linked to one of the cases;
- prepositions which in German require either the accusative, dative or the genitive.

This is explained for each of the four cases in the sections below.

The four cases in more detail

The nominative case

Indicating the subject

As mentioned before, the most important role of the nominative case is to indicate the subject in a sentence. The subject directs the action and can be a person, thing or idea, either in the singular or in the plural:

Der Junge **spielt heute allein.**
The boy is playing alone today.

Die Zeiten **sind hart.**
These are hard times.

A good way of identifying the subject is to ask:

Who or what is doing the action?
– Who is playing alone?
→ The boy.

The nominative after verbs

The nominative is also used after the verbs **sein** 'to be', **werden** 'to become' and **scheinen** 'to seem':

Heinz war immer ein guter Vater.
Heinz was always a good father.

Das Mädchen wird sicher eine berühmte Sängerin werden.
The girl will surely become a famous singer.

Er scheint ein fähiger Trainer zu sein.
He seems to be a capable coach.

Nominative case endings

Here is an overview of the most common determiners in the nominative:

	Masculine	Feminine	Neuter	Plural
Definite article	**der Mann**	**die Tochter**	**das Kind**	**die Leute**
Demonstrative	**dieser Mann**	**diese Tochter**	**dieses Kind**	**diese Leute**
Indefinite article	**ein Mann**	**eine Tochter**	**ein Kind**	**– Leute**
Possessive	**mein Mann**	**meine Tochter**	**mein Kind**	**meine Leute**

The accusative case

Marking the direct object

The accusative case in German marks the direct object in a sentence. The direct object is the person or thing on the receiving end of the action:

Sie füttert *das Baby.*
She feeds the baby.

Helga wäscht *den Wagen.*
Helga washes the car.

In order to identify the direct object, you could ask the question:

At who/m or what is the action directed?
→ The baby.

The accusative after most verbs

Most verbs in German are used with a direct accusative object:

kochen	**Jamie kocht ein Fischgericht.**
schreiben	**Sie schreibt einen Brief.**
vermissen	**Sie vermissen ihre alten Freunde.**

These verbs are called *transitive verbs*. You can find out which verbs are transitive by checking in the dictionary as these verbs are indicated with the letters *vt*.

The accusative after prepositions

The accusative case is always used after the prepositions **bis** 'until', **durch** 'through', **für** 'for', **gegen** 'against', **ohne** 'without', **um** 'round':

Das Geschenk ist nicht für *dich*.
The present is not for you.

Ohne *sein* **Handy verlässt er nie das Haus.**
He never leaves the house without his mobile.

It is also used after **an** 'at', 'on' **auf** 'on', **hinter** 'behind', **in** 'in', '(in)to', **neben** 'next to', **über** 'above', **unter** 'under', **vor** 'before'/'in front of' and **zwischen** 'between' (all of which are called *Wechselpräpositionen*) when movement is implied:

Sie gehen täglich in de*n* **Park.**
They go to the park every day.

Er stellt die Lampe neben *das* **Regal.**
He puts the lamp next to the shelves.

Other triggers – some expressions

The accusative forms are also used after some expressions. They include:

- **es gibt** 'there is'/'there are': **Es gibt keinen Alkohol** 'There is no alcohol';
- greetings and wishes where 'Wishing you a ...', is implied: **Guten Abend!** 'Good evening!'; **Herzlichen Glückwunsch!** 'Congratulations!'.

Accusative case endings

The endings of the most common determiners in the accusative are identical with those in the nominative, apart from the masculine forms, which end in **-en**:

	Masculine		Feminine		Neuter		Plural	
Definite article	**den**	Mann	die	Tochter	das	Kind	die	Leute
Demonstrative	**diesen**	Mann	diese	Tochter	dieses	Kind	diese	Leute
Indefinite article	**einen**	Mann	eine	Tochter	ein	Kind	–	Leute
Possessive	**meinen**	Mann	meine	Tochter	mein	Kind	meine	Leute

The dative case

Indicating the indirect object

In addition to a direct object, many verbs in German can take a further object, the indirect object. The indirect object of a sentence is always in the dative case:

Wir kauften *dem Kind* einen großen Luftballon.
We bought the child a big balloon.

Er macht *der Frau* einen Vorschlag.
He puts a preposition to the woman.

An easy way to identify the indirect object of a sentence is to ask:

To who/m or what is the action being done?
→ The child.

Note that the indirect object in English is often indicated by the preposition 'to' as shown in the above example.

The dative after verbs

Some verbs in German require a dative object. The most common are:
antworten 'to answer', **danken** 'to thank', **folgen** 'to follow', **gehören** 'to belong to', **gratulieren** 'to congratulate', **helfen** 'to help', **schaden** 'to harm', **trauen** 'to trust', **wehtun** 'to hurt':

Bitte antworte *mir*!
Please answer me!

Wir helfen *der* Frau.
We help the woman.

Er traute sein*em* Chef nicht.
He didn't trust his boss.

The dative after prepositions

The dative case is always used after **aus** 'out of', **außer** 'except', **bei** 'at'/'by', **gegenüber** 'opposite', **mit** 'with', **nach** 'after', **seit** 'since', **von** 'from', **zu** 'to':

Das Verkehrsbüro ist gegenüber *dem* Bahnhof.
The tourist information is opposite the station.

Was machst du nach *der* Arbeit?
What are you doing after work?

It also follows the so-called *Wechselpräpositionen* (such as **an** 'at', **auf** 'on' etc.) if the emphasis is on position and not on movement:

Sie machen ein Picknick *im* Park.
They have a picnic in the park.

Die Lampe steht neben d*em* Regal.
The lamp is next to the shelves.

Other triggers – with adjectives

The dative forms are also used in constructions with some adjectives when referring to the person/persons involved:

Sie ist ihr*em* Vater sehr ähnlich.
She is very similar to her father.

Das ist *mir* egal.
That's all the same to me.

Geht es *dir* gut?
Are you well?

Es ist *mir* kalt./*Mir* ist kalt.
I am cold.

Other adjectives which are often used with the dative are: **bekannt** 'known', **fremd** 'strange', **böse** 'angry', **dankbar** 'grateful', **gefährlich** 'dangerous', **schwer** 'heavy'/'difficult'.

Dative case endings

Here is an overview of the most common determiners in the dative:

	Masculine		*Feminine*		*Neuter*		*Plural*	
Definite art.	**dem**	**Mann**	**der**	**Tochter**	**dem**	**Kind**	**den**	**Kindern**
Demonstr.	**diesem**	**Mann**	**dieser**	**Tochter**	**diesem**	**Kind**	**diesen**	**Kindern**
Indefinite art.	**einem**	**Mann**	**einer**	**Tochter**	**einem**	**Kind**	**–**	**Kindern**
Possess.	**meinem**	**Mann**	**meiner**	**Tochter**	**meinem**	**Kind**	**meinen**	**Kindern**

Typical endings for determiners in the dative are:

- **-em**   with masculine and neuter nouns
- **-er**   with feminine nouns and
- **-en**   with nouns in the plural.

Don't forget to add an extra **-(e)n** to the plural form of the noun itself whenever this is possible.

The genitive case

Indicating possession

The genitive case refers to the idea of possession or belonging, corresponding to the English *apostrophe s* (*'s*) ending or the preposition *of*:

Das Auto meines Vaters steht dort drüben.
My father's car is over there.

Wir beginnen mit dem schwierigsten Teil *der* Übersetzung.
We begin with the most difficult part of the translation.

A useful way of recognising the genitive in a sentence is to ask :

Whose . . . is it/are they?
→ My father's.

The genitive with prepositions

The following prepositions require the genitive: **statt** 'instead of', **außerhalb** 'outside of', **innerhalb** 'inside of', **trotz** 'in spite of', **während** 'during' and **wegen** 'due to':

Während *des* Mittagessens sprachen sie über den nächsten Urlaub.
During lunch they talked about the next holiday.

Wegen eines Unfalls kamen wir zu spät.
We were late due to an accident.

Note that in contemporary German these prepositions with the exception of **innerhalb** and **außerhalb** can be used with the *dative* case:

Während dem Mittagessen sprachen sie über den nächsten Urlaub.

Other triggers – some expressions

A few phrases such as **eines Morgens** 'one morning', **eines Sonntags** 'one Sunday', **dieser Tage** 'in the next/last days' are formed with the genitive:

Eines schönen Tages machten sie einen Ausflug in die Berge.
One fine day they went on a trip to the mountains.

Use of the apostrophe

In contrast to English usage, nouns in German with the genitive ending **-s** usually don't take an apostrophe: **Peters neue Freundin kommt aus Brasilien** 'Peter's new girlfriend is from Brazil'.

Genitive case endings

Here is an overview of the typical endings for common determiners and nouns in the genitive:

	Masculine		*Feminine*		*Neuter*		*Plural*	
Definite art.	des	Mannes	der	Tochter	des	Kindes	der	Leute
Demonstr.	dieses	Mannes	dieser	Tochter	dieses	Kindes	dieser	Leute
Indefinite art.	eines	Mannes	einer	Tochter	eines	Kindes	–	Leute
Possess.	meines	Mannes	meiner	Tochter	meines	Kindes	meiner	Leute

Note that in the genitive:

- *masculine* and *neuter* nouns of one syllable usually take the ending -**es**: des **Mann**es, des **Kind**es;
- nouns with two or more syllables normally only add an -**s**: meines **Bruder**s, des **Mittagessen**s;
- *feminine* and *plural* nouns don't take any endings.

Using the dative as an alternative

Although the genitive can still be found in modern German – especially in a more formal context – its use is decreasing. In spoken and sometimes also in written German, the genitive is often replaced with an alternative dative structure:

Das ist die Idee meines Bruders. →
Das ist die Idee *von* mein*em* Bruder.

That is my brother's idea.
That is the idea of my brother.

- For pronouns and cases, see Unit 5.

Exercise 4.1

Identify the function and case of each italicised noun in the following sentences.

> Examples: ***Der Mann* geht ins Kino.**
> Who goes to the cinema?
> → *The man*: subject, nominative
>
> **Das sind die Bücher *meiner Tante*.**
> Whose books are they?
> → *My aunt's*: possession, genitive

1 *Die Studentin* arbeitet am Wochenende bei der Telekom. nom fem, subj
2 *Diese Jacke* habe ich in einer Boutique gekauft. acc- obj
3 Ich rufe *meinen Sohn* in Salzburg an. acc · obj
4 Der Vater schenkt *der Tochter* ein Handy. - dat, ind. obj
5 Hans arbeitet im Geschäft *seines Onkels*. – gen poss
6 Ich möchte am Wochenende *meinen Bruder* besuchen.
7 Wir haben *unserem Chef* eine E-Mail geschrieben. dat ind obj
8 Er repariert den DVD-Spieler *seiner Eltern*. gen poss

Exercise 4.2

Fill in the correct endings of the articles below.

1 Das ist ein___ gute Idee!
2 Heute kommt d___ Onkel auf Besuch.
3 Die Kinder haben ein___ Hund.
4 Erkennen Sie d___ Mann?
5 Er bringt sein___ Freundin Blumen mit.
6 Sie fährt mit d___ Bus nach Hause.
7 Ich stelle die Lampe neben d___ Tisch.
8 Die Schule liegt gegenüber ein___ Kirche.
9 Bitte helfen Sie d___ Frau.
10 Er folgte d___ Auto.
11 Sie ist ihr___ Mutter sehr ähnlich.
12 Sie haben mir ein___ Computer gekauft.
13 Ein___ Morgens wachte er sehr früh auf.
14 Ein___ schönen Tages fuhren sie mit dem Fahrrad an die See.

Exercise 4.3

Rewrite the following sentences by replacing the genitive construction with **von** + dative.

   Example: **Der Motor** *meines Autos* **wird repariert.**
              → **Der Motor** *von meinem* **Auto wird repariert.**

1 Das Büro meines Mannes liegt im Stadtzentrum.
2 Die Managerin meiner Firma kommt aus Stuttgart.
3 Man kann das Drehbuch dieses Spielfilms kaufen.
4 Ich finde das Computerspiel meines Sohnes zu schwer.
5 Er kannte alle Namen der Teilnehmer.

Exercise 4.4

Translate the following sentences into German.

1 This is a car.
2 The car is very expensive.
3 He has a son and a daughter.
4 Do you know the son? (*Use the **du** and **Sie** forms.*)
5 He gives his girlfriend a CD.
6 She bought her brother a bottle of wine.

7   They have a house with a garden.
8   I am cold.
9   It is Peter's birthday.
10 That is my brother's computer.

Checklist	✓
1 Can you name all four cases?	
2 Which case usually refers to the subject? *nom*	
3 Which case is normally used for the direct object *acc* and which one for the indirect object? *dat*	
4 Apart from the function a noun performs in a sentence, what other two main factors can 'trigger' a case? *prepositions verbs*	
5 How is the genitive often substituted? *von + dat*	

UNIT FIVE
Pronouns

What are pronouns?

Pronouns are words that 'stand in' for nouns and refer to persons, things or ideas. The most important ones are the *personal pronouns* (**ich**, **du**, **er/sie/es** etc.):

> **Georg ist noch klein, aber *er* kann schon lesen.**
> Georg is only small but he can already read.

> **Mir gefällt das Auto, aber *es* ist zu teuer.**
> I like the car, but it is too expensive.

Personal and other pronouns

Apart from *personal pronouns* there are several other words that can function as pronouns. In this unit we will deal with:

- *demonstratives* such as **dieser** 'this' etc.;
- *possessives* such as **meine** 'my' etc.; and
- *indefinites* such as **man** 'one'/'you'.

Personal pronouns

Different forms of personal pronouns

Personal pronouns can replace and refer to any kind of noun or noun phrase. They need to agree with the grammatical role of these nouns. This is often indicated by different forms of the pronoun. Here is an overview of personal pronouns in the nominative, accusative and dative case:

Nominative		Accusative		Dative	
ich	I	**mich**	me	**mir**	me
du	you (*inf.*)	**dich**	you	**dir**	you
Sie	you (*form.*)	**Sie**	you	**Ihnen**	you
er	he	**ihn**	him, it	**ihm**	him, it
sie	she	**sie**	her, it	**ihr**	her, it
es	it	**es**	it	**ihm**	it
wir	we	**uns**	us	**uns**	us
ihr	you (*inf.*)	**euch**	you	**euch**	you
Sie	you (*form.*)	**Sie**	you	**Ihnen**	you
sie	they	**sie**	them	**ihnen**	them

Note that the use of pronouns in the *genitive* case is quite rare (see section below).

Personal pronouns in use

The following section shows the usage and different functions of personal pronouns in a sentence.

Pronouns and cases

In the *nominative*, personal pronoun forms refer to the *subject* of the sentence:

Ich gehe nächste Woche in Urlaub.
I am going on holiday next week.

In the *accusative*, they often replace a noun functioning as the direct object:

Kennst du *den Film*?   →   **Nein, ich habe *ihn* noch nicht gesehen.**
Do you know the film?   No, I haven't seen it yet.

They also frequently follow prepositions requiring the accusative:

Für *dich* habe ich immer Zeit.
I've always got time for you.

In the *dative*, personal pronouns can be used used as the *indirect object*, with certain prepositions, some verbs and other structures followed by the dative case:

Er gibt *ihr* einen Schokoriegel.
He gives her a bar of chocolate.

Willst du mit *mir* essen gehen?
Do you want to go out to eat with me?

Kann ich *Ihnen* helfen?
Can I help you?

***Mir* geht es gut.**
I am fine.

The *genitive* forms **meiner** 'mine', **deiner** 'yours'(inf.), **Ihrer** 'yours'(form.), **seiner** his, **ihrer** 'hers', **seiner** 'his', **unser** 'ours', **euer** 'yours'(inf.), **Ihrer** 'yours'(form.), **ihrer** 'theirs' are rarely used in contemporary German. They are usually replaced with an alternative structure:

Wir erinnern uns *seiner*. (*gen.*) →   **Wir erinnern uns an ihn.**
We remember him.   We remember him.

Special use of the pronoun es

Apart from referring to neuter nouns in the nominative and accusative, **es** can also refer to a phrase or a whole sentence:

Sitzen Sie gern in der Sonne?   →   **Ja, ich genieße *es* richtig.**
Do you like sitting in the sun?   Yes, I thoroughly enjoy it.

Position of personal pronouns

In the case of two pronouns functioning as objects in a sentence, the accusative pronoun precedes the dative pronoun:

Wann stellt du mich (*acc.*) ihr (*dat.*) vor?
When will you introduce me to her?

If one of the objects is not a pronoun but a noun the pronoun comes before the noun:

Wann stellst du *mich* deiner Mutter vor?
When will you introduce me to your mother?

Er schenkt *ihr* einen Ring.
He gives her a ring.

Demonstrative pronouns – dieser, der

Demonstrative pronouns refer to specific persons, things or ideas that usually have been mentioned before. There are two types of demonstrative pronouns which are quite similar in meaning: **dieser, diese** etc. and **der**, **die** etc.:

Siehst du die rote Jacke?   →   **Meinst du** *diese*/*die*?
Do you see the red jacket?   Do you mean this one?

These pronouns have to agree in gender, number and case with the noun they replace. Here are all their forms:

	Masculine	Feminine	Neuter	Plural
Nom.	**der**	**die**	**das**	**die**
	dieser	**diese**	**dieses**	**diese**
Acc.	**den**	**die**	**das**	**die**
	diesen	**diese**	**dieses**	**diese**
Dat.	**dem**	**der**	**dem**	**denen**
	diesem	**dieser**	**diesem**	**diesen**
Gen.	**dessen**	**deren**	**dessen**	**deren**
	dieses	**dieser**	**dieses**	**dieser**

Note that the adverbs **hier** 'here', **da** 'here'/'there', **dort** 'there'/'over there' are often added for clarification.

Möchten Sie diesen/den hier mitnehmen?
Would you like to take that one (here)?

Diese/die da hab ich noch nie gesehen.
These I have never seen before.

Indefinite pronouns – man, alle, viele **etc.**

Indefinite pronouns refer to persons, things or ideas that are not closely identified. The most commonly used indefinite pronoun is **man**.

Referring to people in a general sense – man

The pronoun **man** 'one' is used to refer to people/they or you in a general sense. It is mainly used in the nominative, as the subject of a sentence or clause:

Man tut das nicht.
You don't do that./One does not do that.

Man sagt, dass Paris romantisch ist.
They say that Paris is romantic.

Occasionally, **man** can also appear as a direct or indirect object. Its accusative and dative forms are **einen** and **einem**:

Acc.   **Manche Ärzte behandeln *einen* wie ein Kind.**
         Some doctors treat you/people like children.

Dat.   **Was sie ein*em* alles verkaufen wollen!**
         The things they try to sell you/people!

Referring to groups of people – alle, viele

The pronouns **alle** 'all, everyone' and **viele** 'many' are normally used to refer to a group of people:

Nom.   **Alle haben gelacht.**
         Everyone laughed.

Acc.   **Sie mochte alle.**
         She liked all of them.

Dat.   **Er redete mit vielen.**
         He talked to many of them.

Note that **alle** and **viele** take the same plural endings as the pronoun **dieser** (see page 37).

Referring to things and ideas only – alles, etwas and nichts

Some pronouns in English and German refer to things and ideas only. The most important are **alles** 'everything', **etwas** 'something', **nichts** 'nothing':

Alles war zu teuer.
Everything was too expensive.

Mach doch etwas!
Do something!

Sie glaubt an nichts.
She doesn't believe in anything.

Possessive pronouns

Possessives, indicating ownership, can also function as pronouns:

Ist das *Ihr Buch*?   →   **Ja, das ist *meins*.**
Habt ihr *eure Joggingschuhe* mit?   **Ja, wir haben *unsere* mit.**

Possessive pronouns have to agree in gender, number and case with the noun they refer to. As an example here are all forms of **meiner** 'mine':

	Masculine	Feminine	Neuter	Plural
Nom.	mein**er**	mein**e**	mein**s**	mein**e**
Acc.	mein**en**	mein**e**	mein**s**	mein**e**
Dat.	mein**em**	mein**er**	mein**em**	mein**en**
Gen.	mein**es**	mein**er**	mein**es**	mein**er**

The above endings are also added to the basic forms of all other possessives **dein-**, **Ihr-**, **sein-**, **ihr-**, **sein-**, **unser-**, **eu(e)r-**, **Ihr-** and **ihr-**.

Other pronouns

Other types of pronouns include *reflexive pronouns*, *relative pronouns* and the *negative* **keiner**. For more information see Unit 6, Unit 20 and Unit 21 respectively.

Exercise 5.1

Complete the following sentences by filling in the correct personal pronoun in the nominative.

> Example: **Der Computer kostet sehr viel, aber _____ ist der beste.**
> → **Der Computer kostet sehr viel, aber *er* ist der beste.**

1 Unser Auto ist nicht hier, weil ___ in der Garage steht.
2 Du hast doch einen Garten. Ist ___ groß?
3 Wir möchten bitte diese Suppe, aber ___ muss heiß sein!
4 Ich mag mein Haus, nur ist ___ leider zu klein.
5 Die Schuhe passen gut und außerdem waren ___ billig.
6 Wie viel hat der Laptop gekostet und wird ___ noch verkauft?

Exercise 5.2

Answer the following questions and replace the nouns with a personal pronoun in the nominative, accusative or dative as appropriate.

Example:
Versteht der Kandidat die Fragen? → **Ja, _____ versteht _____ .**
Versteht der Kandidat die Fragen? → **Ja, *er* versteht *sie*.**

1 Kennt deine Schwester den Popstar? → Ja, _sie_ kennt _ihn_ .

2 Ist das Geschenk für meine Mutter?   Ja, _es_ ist für _ihr_ .

3 Essen Sie den Kuchen ganz auf?   Ja, _sie_ esse _es_ ganz auf.

4 Haben die Leute der Trainerin gedankt?   Ja, _Sie_ haben _ihr_ gedankt.

5 Gefällt die Kette dem Kunden?   Ja, _es_ gefällt _es_ .

6 Helfen die Kinder immer ihren Eltern?   Ja, _Sie_ helfen _ihnen_ immer.

Exercise 5.3

Replace the noun with the appropriate form of the possessive pronoun.

Example: **Das ist das Fahrrad von Martin.** → **Das ist _____ .**
          Das ist das Fahrrad von Martin. → **Das ist *seins*.**

1 Wir nehmen das Auto von mir.   → Wir nehmen _____ .
2 Ist das Bettinas Tasche?   Ja, das ist _____ .
3 Ist das Arnolds Mantel?   Ja, das ist _____ .
4 Das ist der Computer von Steffi.   Das ist _____ .
5 Sind das die Bücher von dir?   Ja, das sind _____ .
6 Das sind Susis und Margrets Bücher.   Das sind _____ .

Exercise 5.4

Translate the following sentences into German.

1 The book was interesting but it was too long.
2 Do you know the film? I don't know it. (*Use the* **Sie** *form.*)
3 The present is for him.

4 He gives her a Ferrari.
5 The bottle of champagne is from us.
6 Do you see the blue jacket? – Do you mean this one?
   (*Use the **Sie** form.*)
7 You don't do that.
8 They say that Vienna is romantic.
9 Everyone laughed.
10 Many came to the party.

Checklist	✓
1 What is the function of a pronoun?	
2 Why do personal pronouns often exist in different forms?	
3 Can you list all personal pronouns in the accusative and dative case?	
4 Can you remember the forms of the demonstrative pronoun **dieser**?	

UNIT SIX
Reflexive verbs

What are reflexive verbs?

Reflexive verbs refer to an action where the subject of a sentence is doing something to itself:

Ich habe mich verletzt.
I have hurt myself.

Marco amüsiert sich.
Marco enjoys himself.

Reflexive verbs are always used with a reflexive pronoun (**mich**, **sich** etc.) which reflects the action back to the subject of the sentence.

Two types of reflexive verbs

There are two main types of reflexive verbs in German:

- 'true' reflexive verbs such as **sich bedanken** 'to say thank you', **sich verabschieden** 'to say goodbye', which can *only* be used reflexively; and
- a large group of verbs, which are usually used in a non-reflexive way but can also function reflexively:

Non-reflexive		*Reflexive*
Ich *wasche* **das Asuto.**	→	**Ich** *wasche* **mich.**
I wash the car.		I wash myself./I have a wash.

Both types of reflexive verbs are usually used with an accusative pronoun (**mich** etc.) but can also be accompanied by a dative reflexive pronoun (**mir** etc.).

Reflexive pronouns in the accusative and dative

Here is an overview of the reflexive pronouns in the accusative and dative:

Accusative	Dative		Accusative	Dative	
mich	mir	myself	uns	uns	ourselves
dich	dir	yourself (*inf.*)	euch	euch	yourselves (*inf.*)
sich	sich	yourself (*form.*)	sich	sich	yourselves (*form.*)
sich	sich	himself/itself			
sich	sich	herself/itself	sich	sich	themselves
sich	sich	itself			

Note that only the **ich** and **du** forms of the accusative and dative differ (**mich/mir** and **dich/dir**).

'True' reflexive verbs + accusative

Here are some commonly used 'true' reflexive verbs that are always used with an accusative reflexive pronoun:

sich amüsieren	to amuse oneself
sich bedanken	to say thank you
sich beeilen	to hurry (up)
sich befinden	to be/to be situated
sich benehmen	to behave
sich entschließen	to decide
sich erkälten	to catch a cold
sich erholen	to recuperate, relax
sich irren	to be mistaken/wrong
sich verabschieden	to take one's leave
sich verletzen	to hurt oneself
sich verlieben	to fall in love
sich verspäten	to be late
sich weigern	to refuse

Here are some of them in use:

Ich möchte *mich* für das Geschenk bedanken.
I'd like to say thank you for the present.

Bitte beeil *dich*!
Please hurry up!

Wir erholen *uns* am liebsten beim Schwimmen.
Our favourite way to relax is to go swimming.

'True' reflexive verbs + dative

There are also a few 'true' reflexive verbs that need a reflexive pronoun in the dative. The most important are:

sich aneignen	to learn/acquire
sich einbilden	to get hold of an idea
sich verbitten	not to tolerate something
sich vornehmen	to intend to do
sich vorstellen	to imagine something
sich überlegen	to think something over

Here are some of them in use:

Überleg *dir* das noch mal!
Think it over again!

Ich habe *mir* fest vorgenommen mit dem Rauchen aufzuhören.
I firmly intend to stop smoking.

Stellt *euch* vor, ihr seid im Amazonas!
Imagine you are in the Amazon!

Remember that the reflexive dative pronouns only differ from the accusative in the first and second person singular: **ich** → *mir* and **du** → *dir*.

Other verbs used reflexively

Verbs with an accusative object

Many verbs taking an accusative object can also be used reflexively when it relates the action back to the subject:

With an accusative object		*Reflexive*
Er möchte *die Welt* ändern.	→	**Er möchte *sich* ändern.**
He wants to change the world.		He wants to change (himself).

Wir waschen *das Auto*.	**Wir waschen *uns*.**
We wash the car.	We wash ourselves./
	We have a wash.

Other frequently used verbs of this type are: **sich anziehen** 'to get dressed', **sich setzen** 'to sit down', **sich fragen** 'to ask oneself', **sich vorbereiten** 'to prepare oneself', **sich vorstellen** 'to introduce oneself'.

Verbs with a dative object

Many verbs that require a dative object can be used with a dative reflexive pronoun if the action focuses on the subject itself:

With a dative object	*Reflexive*
Ich werde dem Kind helfen. →	**Ich werde mir selbst helfen.**
I will help the child.	I will help myself.
Du schadest der Umwelt.	**Damit schadest du dir.**
You are harming the environment.	You are harming yourself with that.

Other verbs belonging to this group are: **sich widersprechen** 'to contradict oneself', **sich erlauben** 'to allow oneself something', **sich leisten** 'to be able to afford something', **sich zumuten** 'to ask something of oneself'.

Reflexive verbs + prepositions

A number of reflexive verbs are normally used together with a preposition, such as **sich erinnern** + **an** or **sich interessieren** + **für**:

Sie erinnert *sich* an ihren ersten Freund.
She remembers her first boyfriend.

Interessiert ihr *euch* für Fußball?
Are you interested in football?

Other examples include: **sich ärgern über** 'to be annoyed about', **sich aufregen über** 'to be upset, angry about', **sich beschweren über/bei** 'to complain about/to', **sich freuen auf** 'to look forward to', **sich freuen über** 'to be happy about/with'.

For more information, see Unit 9.

Structures with accusative *and* dative objects

In structures where the reflexive verb occurs with an accusative and dative object, the reflexive pronoun is usually in the dative:

Ich habe *mir* (*dat.*) **den Rücken** (*acc.*) **verletzt.**
I've hurt my back.

Ich ziehe *mir* (*dat.*) **den Mantel** (*acc.*) **an.**
I put on my coat.

Wasch *dir* (*dat.*) **bitte die Hände!** (*acc.*)
Wash your hands, please!

Wir haben *uns* (*dat.*) **die Zähne** (*acc.*) **geputzt.**
We (have) cleaned our teeth.

As shown in these examples, in English these structures usually use a possessive adjective ('my', 'your' etc.) instead of a reflexive pronoun.

Position of the reflexive pronoun

If the subject is a noun

If the subject is a noun, the reflexive pronoun usually appears *after* the *finite verb*:

Seine kleine Schwester *interessiert sich* **für Rapmusik.**
His younger sister is interested in rap music.

In a subordinate clause the reflexive pronoun usually comes *before* the *subject*:

Es ist klar, dass *sich Claudia* **entschuldigen muss.**
It is clear that Claudia has to apologise.

If the subject is a personal pronoun

If the subject is a personal pronoun the reflexive pronoun often appears *after* the *subject*:

Gestern hat *sie sich* **von dem Schrecken erholt.**
She recovered from the shock yesterday.

However, if the sentence starts with a pronoun as the subject the reflexive pronoun is placed *after* the *finite verb*:

Er *sollte sich* mal rasieren.
He should have a shave.

In the imperative

The reflexive pronoun usually appears *after* the *personal pronoun*:

Bedanken *wir uns*!
Let's say thank you!

Stellen *Sie sich* das vor!
Imagine that!

With the **du** and **ihr** imperative forms the reflexive pronoun appears *after* the *finite verb*:

***Zieh dir* die Jacke an!**
Put on your jacket!

***Benehmt euch*!**
Behave yourselves!

Exercise 6.1

Decide if the following reflexive verbs are used with a reflexive pronoun in the accusative or the dative by putting them in the appropriate column below. The first one has been done for you.

> **sich amüsieren   sich bedanken   sich beeilen**
> **sich erholen   sich entschließen   sich erkälten   sich überlegen**
> **sich verlieben   sich verspäten   sich verabschieden**
> **sich verletzen   sich vornehmen**

Reflexive pronoun in the accusative	*Reflexive pronoun in the dative*
sich amüsieren	

Exercise 6.2

Fill in the gaps in the following sentences with the appropriate accusative or dative reflexive pronoun.

> Example: **Ich bedanke _____ für das Geschenk.**
> → **Ich bedanke** *mich* **für das Geschenk.**

1 Er interessiert *sich* sehr für Fußball.
2 Du erinnerst *dich* sicher nicht mehr an die Party vor fünf Jahren.
3 Ich muss *mich* beeilen.
4 Wir erholen *uns* immer gut in den Bergen.
5 Hoffentlich überlegst du *dich* das noch!
6 Du solltest *dich* jeden Tag zweimal die Zähne putzen.
7 Ich habe nicht bemerkt, dass ich *mich* beim Trainieren verletzt habe.

Exercise 6.3

Construct complete sentences using the information given below, starting with the element in italics.

> Example: **verabschiedeten/uns/von unseren Freunden/*wir***
> → **Wir verabschiedeten uns von unseren Freunden.**

1 ihren Bruder/sich/über/ärgert/*sie* *sie ärgert sich über ihren Bruder*
2 damit/schaden/uns/können/*wir* *wir können uns damit schaden*
3 hat/Marco/*gestern*/verliebt/sich *gestern hat Marco sich verliebt*
4 wegen der Panne/hat/sich/verspätet/*er* *er hat sich wegen der Panne verspätet*
5 gut/*vor ihren Eltern*/sie/sich/benehmen *vor ihren Eltern benehmen sie sich gut*
6 *überlegt*/noch mal/euch/das *überlegt das euch noch mal*

Exercise 6.4

Translate the following sentences into German.

1 I would like to apologise.
2 We want to say thank you for the present.
3 Are you interested in sport? (*Use the **du**, **Sie** and **ihr** forms.*)
4 Have you hurt yourself? (*Use the **du**, **Sie** and **ihr** forms.*)
5 I clean my teeth very often.

6 I put on my shoes.
7 We should ask ourselves this question.
8 Imagine that! (*Use the **du**, **Sie** and **ihr** forms.*)

Checklist	✓
1 Can you explain what a 'true' reflexive verb is?	
2 Do you know the reflexive pronouns in the accusative?	
3 Which reflexive pronouns in the dative differ from those in the accusative?	
4 What is the position of the reflexive pronoun when the subject is a noun?	

UNIT SEVEN
Modal verbs

Modal verbs – expressing ability, necessity etc.

Modal verbs modify an action or situation by expressing the idea of ability, obligation, permission etc.:

> **Sie *kann* sehr gut schwimmen.** She can swim very well.
> **Wir *müssen* jetzt gehen.** We have to go now.
> **Hier *dürfen* Sie rauchen.** You are allowed to smoke here.

Modal verbs in German

In German there are six modal verbs:

dürfen	may/to be allowed to
können	can/to be able to
mögen	to like (to) (also used in the form **möchten**).
müssen	must/to have to
sollen	to be supposed to/should/ought to
wollen	to want to

Meaning and most common usage

dürfen – *permission, prohibition ('must not')*

dürfen usually conveys the idea of permission and can be translated with 'may'/'can' or 'to be allowed to':

> **Darf ich hier fotografieren?**
> Am I allowed to take photos here?

Hier dürfen Sie parken.
You can/are allowed to park here.

It often adds a sense of politeness and can be used in more formal situations:

Darf ich Ihnen behilflich sein?
May I help you?

When used in the negative, **dürfen** expresses prohibition ('must not', 'not to be allowed to'):

Das dürfen Sie nicht.
You must not do this.

Als Kind durfte sie nie fernsehen.
As a child she was never allowed to watch TV.

können – *ability*

können corresponds to the English 'can' or 'to be able to' and usually expresses ability:

Du kannst morgen kommen.
You can come tomorrow.

Er konnte sehr gut surfen.
He could surf very well.

It can sometimes add a tone of possibility as in the English 'may':

Das kann schon wahr sein.
This may be true.

mögen – *inclination, liking*

mögen implies that people like something generally:

Sie mag italienischen Wein.
She likes Italian wine.

Wir mögen klassische Musik.
We like classical music.

Note that **mögen** can only be used in structures with *nouns* or *noun phrases*. In connection with *verb structures*, **gern** has to be used: **Sie *trinkt gern* italienischen Wein. Wir *hören gern* klassische Musik.**

mögen is frequently used in its subjunctive form, **möchten** 'would like':

Ich möchte einen Cappuccino.
I would like a cappuccino.

Was möchtest du machen?
What would you like to do?

For more details on the different forms of **möchten**, see Unit 23.

müssen – *necessity, obligation*

müssen usually expresses a sense of necessity or obligation and corresponds to the English 'must' or 'to have to':

Wir müssen jetzt gehen.
We must/have to go now.

Sie muss das Projekt bis Anfang September fertig haben.
She must/has to finish the project by the beginning of September.

In the *negative*, **müssen** does not convey the meaning of prohibition as it does in English, but means 'don't have to' or 'don't need to':

Ihr müsst jetzt noch nicht gehen.
You don't have to/don't need to go now.

Du musst dir keine Sorgen machen.
You don't have to/don't need to worry.

Note that in these contexts **brauchen** is often used as an alternative:

Ihr braucht jetzt noch nicht zu gehen.
You don't need to/have to go now.

sollen – *obligations, commands*

sollen is mainly used to convey a sense of obligation and corresponds to the English 'be supposed to', 'should':

Peter soll fettarmer essen.
Peter is supposed to eat less fat.

Ich soll heute meine Mutter anrufen.
I am supposed to ring my mother today.

It is also used with suggestions or commands:

Sollen wir mit dem Auto fahren?
Should we go by car?

Du sollst dich schämen!
You should be ashamed (of yourself)!

sollen can also convey a sense of uncertainty when making a prediction or when reporting what you have heard from another source:

Morgen soll es regnen.
Rain is forecast for tomorrow.

Sie soll wieder geheiratet haben.
They say she's got married again.

wollen – *intention, desire*

wollen usually expresses an intention or desire and corresponds to the English 'to want to':

Ich will mit dem Rauchen aufhören.
I want to stop smoking.

Gaby will auswandern.
Gaby wants to emigrate.

Formation in different tenses

Modal verbs are quite irregular in German. Here is a summary of their forms in different tenses.

Present tense

In the present tense only **sollen** doesn't change its stem vowel in the **ich**, **du** and **er/sie/es** forms. Note also that the first and third person singular (**ich** and **er/sie/es**) have identical forms and don't have their usual present tense endings.

	dürfen	*können*	*mögen*	*müssen*	*sollen*	*wollen*
ich	darf	kann	mag	muss	soll	will
du	darfst	kannst	magst	musst	sollst	willst
~~Sie~~	~~dürfen~~	~~können~~	~~mögen~~	~~müssen~~	~~sollen~~	~~wollen~~
er/sie/es	darf	kann	mag	muss	soll	will
wir	dürfen	können	mögen	müssen	sollen	wollen
ihr	dürft	könnt	mögt	müsst	sollt	wollt
Sie	dürfen	können	mögen	müssen	sollen	wollen
sie	dürfen	können	mögen	müssen	sollen	wollen

Present perfect tense

The *past participle* of the six modals are: **gedurft, gekonnt, gemocht, gemusst, gesollt, gewollt**.

However, these forms are rarely used and are usually replaced with the simple past forms of the modals:

present perfect	**Sie hat den Film nicht gemocht.** →
simple past	**Sie mochte den Film nicht.**
	She didn't like the film.

When the modal appears together with another verb, the present perfect tense is constructed with **haben** + *infinitive* of the *second verb* + *infinitive of the modal*:

Hugo hat noch bis spät arbeiten müssen.
Hugo (has) had to work late.

Eva hat noch einen Kaffee trinken wollen.
Eva wanted to drink another coffee.

Note that as the infinitive of the modal verb is used instead of the past participle form, the sentence finishes in two infinitives (double infinitive construction). This present perfect structure is often avoided by using the simple past tense: **Hugo musste noch bis spät arbeiten** → **Eva wollte noch einen Kaffee trinken**.

Simple past tense

Modal verbs form their simple past tense by dropping the umlaut and by using **-te** endings:

	dürfen	*können*	*mögen*	*müssen*	*sollen*	*wollen*
ich	durfte	konnte	mochte	musste	sollte	wollte
du	durftest	konntest	mochtest	musstest	solltest	wolltest
Sie	durften	konnten	mochten	mussten	sollten	wollten
er/sie/es	durfte	konnte	mochte	musste	sollte	wollte
wir	durften	konnten	mochten	mussten	sollten	wollten
ihr	durftet	konntet	mochtet	musstet	solltet	wolltet
Sie	durften	konnten	mochten	mussten	sollten	wollten
sie	durften	konnten	mochten	mussten	sollten	wollten

Sie durfte nicht ins Kino gehen.
he was not allowed to go to the cinema.

Er konnte sehr gut tanzen.
He could dance very well.

Wolltest du etwas fragen?
Did you want to ask something?

Wir mochten die Musik nicht.
We didn't like the music.

Past perfect tense

If the modal verb stands on its own, the past perfect tense is constructed with the past tense of **haben** + *the past participle* of the modal. When the modal verb appears together with another verb, the past perfect tense is constructed with the *infinitive* of the *second verb* + *the infinitive form* of the *modal*:

Er hatte das nicht gewollt.
He had not wanted this.

Ich hatte Tom Hanks interviewen dürfen.
I had been allowed to interview Tom Hanks.

Future tense

The future tense of modal verbs is constructed with the finite form of **werden** + the *infinitive* of the *main verb* + *the infinitive* of the *modal*:

Pavarotti wird nicht singen können.
Pavarotti won't be able to sing.

Sie wird ein neues Auto kaufen müssen.
She will have to buy a new car.

Modal verbs used without another verb

Although modal verbs frequently appear in connection with another verb, they can also stand on their own. This is often the case in colloquial phrases:

Ich kann nicht mehr.	I can't go on anymore./ I've had enough.
Wir müssen jetzt nach Hause.	We have to go home now.
Wir wollen in die Stadt.	We want to go/drive into town.
Er kann das sehr gut.	He can do this very well.
Das darfst du nicht.	You are not allowed to do this.
Können Sie Deutsch?	Can you speak German?
Was soll das?	What's this supposed to mean?

- For details on the position of modal verbs in various sentence structures, see Unit 19.

Exercise 7.1

Fill in the appropriate form of the modal verb in the present tense. You will find the infinitives in brackets.

> Example: **Er _____ ab sofort mit dem Rauchen aufhören. (sollen)**
> → **Er *soll* ab sofort mit dem Rauchen aufhören.**

1 Die Kinder _dürfen_ nur bis 9 Uhr aufbleiben. (dürfen)
2 Er _kann_ an dieser Situation beim besten Willen nichts ändern. (können)
3 Meine Großmutter _müssen_ ins Krankenhaus. (müssen)
4 Ich _mag_ unsere neue Kollegin überhaupt nicht. (mögen)
5 Warum _will_ Ihre Tochter nicht im Ausland studieren? (wollen)
6 Du _darfst_ keinen Alkohol mehr trinken. (dürfen)
7 Wann _müsst_ ihr nach Hause? (müssen)
8 Schade, dass ihr nicht mitkommen _könnt_ . (können)

Exercise 7.2

Now put all the sentences of Exercise 7.1 into the simple past tense.

Example: **Er *sollte* ab sofort keinen Alkohol mehr trinken.**

Exercise 7.3

Convert the following sentences into the present perfect by using two infinitives.

Examples: **Wir kamen zur Party. (können)**
    → **Wir haben zur Party *kommen können.***

Er fuhr ins Ausland. (wollen)
    → **Er hat ins Ausland *fahren wollen.***

1 Der Sänger rauchte nicht. (dürfen) *Der Sänger hat nicht rauchen dürfen*
2 Ich trieb mehr Sport. (wollen) *Ich habe mehr Sport treiben wollen*
3 Sie arbeiteten in der Nacht. (müssen) *Sie haben in der Nacht arbeiten müssen*
4 Er interviewte Al Pacino. (dürfen) *Er hat Al Pacino interviewen dürfen*
5 Wir flogen nach Miami. (können) *Wir haben nach Miami fliegen können*

Exercise 7.4

Translate the sentences below into German.

1 She likes classical music. *Sie mag klassische Musik*
2 Shall we go by car? *Sollen wir bis Auto fahren*
3 You are allowed to park here. (*Use the du, Sie and ihr forms.*) *Du darfst nicht hier parken*
4 He is supposed to eat more fruit. *Er soll mehr Obst essen*
5 The children must not watch television. *Die Kinder muss nicht Fern sehen*
6 She wasn't allowed to go to the cinema. *Sie durfte nicht ins Kino gehen*
7 They had to go home. *Sie mussten nach Hause gehen*
8 You must not do that! (*Use the du, Sie and ihr forms.*) *Sie müssen das nicht machen*
9 The band won't be able to play. *Der Band kann nicht spielen*
10 We will have to buy a new radio. *Wir werden ein neues Radio kaufen müssen*
11 Can you speak Italian? (*Use the du, Sie and ihr forms.*) *Kannst du Italienisch sprechen*
12 What is this supposed to mean? *Was soll es meinen*

Checklist	✓
1 Can you name the infinitive forms of the six modal verbs in German?	
2 Can you give the German translation of the expression 'I must not . . .'?	
3 How do modal verbs form their simple past tense?	
4 Can you give four examples where a modal verb is used without another verb?	

UNIT EIGHT
Verbs with separable and inseparable prefixes

Different types of prefixes

Many verbs in German consist of a main verb and a prefix: ***an*kommen** 'to arrive', ***ver*kaufen** 'to sell', ***über*setzen** 'to translate'/'to ferry over'.

There are three different types of prefixes in German:

- *separable* prefixes which – as the name suggests – can exist separately from the main verb;
- *inseparable* prefixes which are fixed to the verb;
- *variable* prefixes which can either be separable or inseparable.

Here are all three forms in more detail.

Separable verbs

List of commonly used separable prefixes

Separable verbs are used frequently in German. Here is a list of common prefixes together with one possible combination as an example:

ab-	**abfahren**	to depart (by vehicle)
an-	**anrufen**	to telephone
auf-	**aufmachen**	to open
aus-	**ausgehen**	to go out
bei-	**beitreten**	to join (an organisation)
ein-	**einkaufen**	to shop
fest-	**festnehmen**	to take into custody
her-	**herkommen**	to come (from somewhere)
hin-	**hinsetzen**	to sit down

mit-	mitmachen	to join in
statt-	stattfinden	to take place
vor-	vorbereiten	to prepare
weg-	wegbringen	to take away
zu-	zulegen	to put on
zurück-	zurückgeben	to return (something)
zusammen-	zusammenzählen	to add up

Here are some of them in use:

Sie gehen heute Abend aus.
They are going out tonight.

Die Wahlen fanden letzten September statt.
The election took place last September.

Hast du schon die DVDs zurückgegeben?
Have you returned the DVDs?

Separable verbs do not always split up

Separable verbs can – as the name indicates – split into two parts. However, they also appear as one word in certain constructions.

When to separate
A separable verb splits when it is the only verb in a *main clause*. This applies to the following structures. Note that the prefix appears in the final position:

present tense	**Er *ruft* seine Freundin um 8 Uhr *an*.**
	He calls his girlfriend at 8 o'clock.
simple past tense	**Ich *kam* am Dienstag *zurück*.**
	I returned on Tuesday.
imperative	**Steh sofort *auf*!**
	Get/Stand up at once!

When not to separate
Separable verbs appear as one word and in the infinitive with *modal verbs* and the *future tense*:

Er muss seine Freundin *anrufen*.
He has to call his girlfriend.

Ich werde am Dienstag *zurückkommen.*
I'll return on Tuesday.

In most *subordinate clauses*, the separable verb moves to the last position and does not split up. Its ending must agree with the subject of the clause:

Sag mir, wann du *ankommst.*
Tell me when you'll arrive.

Ich verstehe nicht, warum er sich immer so *aufregt.*
I don't understand why he always gets so upset.

Past participles

The past participle of separable verbs is normally formed by inserting -**ge**- between the prefix and the main verb: **ankommen → an*ge*kommen**.

For more detail on the formation of past participles and their usage in the present perfect and past perfect tense, see Units 11 and 13.

Verbs with inseparable prefixes

List of commonly used inseparable prefixes

There are also a number of prefixes which never detach themselves from the main verb. They include:

be-	**besuchen**	to visit
emp-	**empfinden**	to feel
ent-	**entleeren**	to empty
er-	**erzählen**	to tell (a story)
ge-	**gehören**	to belong
miss-	**missachten**	to disregard
ver-	**verlieren**	to lose
zer-	**zerstören**	to destroy

Here are some of them in use:

Sie besuchen ihre Eltern fast jedes Wochenende.
They visit their parents almost every weekend.

Erzähl uns noch eine Geschichte!
Tell us another story!

Dieses Buch gehört Martin.
This book belongs to Martin.

Past participles

Verbs with inseparable prefixes *don't* add **ge-** when forming their past participle:

Sie hat das nicht bereut.
She hasn't regretted it.

Paul hat gestern seinen Pass verloren.
Paul lost his passport yesterday.

Verbs with variable prefixes

There are also some prefixes which can either be separable or inseparable. They include:

durch-	**durchlassen** (*sep.*)	to let through
	durchdenken (*insep.*)	to think through
über-	**überkochen** (*sep.*)	to boil over
	übernachten (*insep.*)	to stay overnight
um-	**umfallen** (*sep.*)	to fall over
	umarmen (*insep.*)	to embrace
unter-	**untergehen** (*sep.*)	to sink
	unterrichten (*insep.*)	to teach
wieder-	**wiedersehen** (*sep.*)	to see again
	wiederholen (*insep.*)	to repeat
wider-	**widerspiegeln** (*sep.*)	to reflect
	widersprechen (*insep.*)	to contradict

Here are some of them in use:

Die Suppe kochte über.
The soup was boiling over.

Sie übernachteten in einem Hotel.
They stayed overnight in a hotel.

Das Schiff ist untergegangen.
The ship has sunk.

Er hat früher Physik unterrichtet.
He used to teach physics.

How to spot the difference

A way of identifying a separable or inseparable prefix is to see where the stress falls:

- if the verb is separable, the stress usually falls on the prefix: ***durch*fallen**, ***über*kochen**, ***um*fallen**, ***unter*gehen**, ***wieder*sehen**, ***wider*spiegeln**;
- if the verb is inseparable, the stress falls on the main verb: **durch*denken***, **über*nachten***, **um*armen***, **unter*richten***, **wieder*holen***, **wider*sprechen***.

Same word, different meanings

A few verbs exist as a separable as well as an inseparable verb. Although the prefix is the same, their meaning and stress differ:

Separable		Inseparable	
***über*setzen**	to ferry across	**über*setzen***	to translate
***über*ziehen**	to put/pull on	**über*ziehen***	to overdraw (account)
***um*schreiben**	to rewrite	**um*schreiben***	to paraphrase

The above separable forms often convey the literal meaning of the verb, while the inseparable forms usually have a more figurative meaning:

Das Boot setzt über.	The boat ferries across.
Marco übersetzt einen Text.	Marco is translating a text.
Sie hat ihre Jacke übergezogen.	She has put on her jacket.
Sie hat ihr Konto überzogen.	She has overdrawn her account.

Verbs can have various prefixes

Note that many verbs in German can exist with various prefixes, such as the verb **arbeiten**:

***auf*arbeiten** (*sep.*)	to do up, to reappraise (the past)
***aus*arbeiten** (*sep.*)	to work out

bearbeiten (*insep.*)	to deal with, to revise
einarbeiten (*sep.*)	to get used to the work, to train
erarbeiten (*insep.*)	to work for, to acquire
mitarbeiten (*sep.*)	to cooperate
überarbeiten (*insep.*)	to rework, to overwork
umarbeiten (*sep.*)	to rewrite, to rework
zusammenarbeiten (*sep.*)	to cooperate, to work together

Learning tip

Memorising a verb together with its separable and inseparable prefixes – preferably as part of a phrase or sentence – can help you to extend your vocabulary.

If you are not sure whether a verb is separable, look it up in the dictionary. Separable verbs are usually indicated with the abbreviation *sep.*

Exercise 8.1

Indicate if the following verbs are either separable (*sep.*) or inseparable (*insep.*) and give their main meaning in English.

Examples: **anrufen** → **anrufen** (*sep.*)   to telephone
          erzählen → **erzählen** (*insep.*)   to tell (a story)

1 abfahren, 2 anfangen, 3 aufschreiben, 4 aufhören, 5 ausgehen,
6 berichten, 7 bezahlen, 8 einladen, 9 entstehen, 10 entwerfen,
11 erlauben, 12 erfinden, 13 festmachen, 14 gehören, 15 gewinnen,
16 hinfallen, 17 mitmachen, 18 mitgehen, 19 stattfinden, 20 übernachten,
21 umarmen, 22 umtauschen, 23 verlieren, 24 vorstellen, 25 wegfahren,
26 wiedersehen, 27 wiederholen, 28 zumachen.

Exercise 8.2

Find the right prefixes for the separable verbs from the box below and use them to complete the sentences.

> fest an aus wieder um vor an auf unter

Example:

Der Gast kommt am Dienstag um 9 Uhr im Hotel _____ .
→ **Der Gast kommt am Dienstag um 9 Uhr im Hotel *an*.**

1 Sie gehen jedes Wochenende _unter_ .
2 Das Konzert fängt um 8 Uhr ___an___ .   an
3 Ich sehe ihn bald _wieder_ .
4 Tanja und Leo bereiten sich auf die Englischprüfung ___vor___ .
5 Der Polizist nimmt die Verbrecher ___fest___ .
6 Ich höre mit dem Rauchen ___auf___ . auf
7 Das Boot geht niemals ___aus___ . aus
8 Der Politiker schreibt die Rede noch einmal ___um___ . um

Exercise 8.3

Now transform each of the sentences in Exercise **8.2** into subordinate clauses by starting the sentences with **Ich bin sicher, dass . . . .** Don't forget that the separable verb does not split up in this construction.

Example:

Der Gast _kommt_ am Dienstag um 9 Uhr im Hotel _an_.
→ **Ich bin sicher, dass der Gast am Dienstag um 9 Uhr im Hotel _ankommt_.**

Exercise 8.4

Translate the sentences below into German.

1 I often go out.
2 She calls her sister in Germany.
3 He teaches mathematics.
4 We visit our parents every month.
5 Max has to prepare for the meeting.
6 Open the door! (*Use the **du** and **Sie** forms.*)
7 The milk is boiling over.
8 I'm staying overnight at the Hilton.
9 They repeat the word three times.
10 I think that the film starts at 8 o'clock.

Checklist	✓
1 What are the three different types of prefixes?	
2 Can you list five prefixes that never separate from the verb?	
3 How do you form a past participle of a separable verb and an inseparable verb?	
4 How can you find out whether a verb is separable or inseparable?	

UNIT NINE
Verbs and prepositions

Verbs and prepositions in English and German

In German as in English many verbs are followed by a preposition:

> **Wir sprechen *über* den Film.**
> We talk *about* the film.

> **Sie entschuldigt sich *für* die Verspätung.**
> She apologises for the delay.

Although German prepositions used in connection with a verb might sometimes correspond to the English as with **sprechen *über*** 'to talk *about*', there is often no correlation between the two languages:

> **Ich warte *auf* den Bus.**
> I am waiting *for* the bus.

> **Sie entschuldigt sich *bei* ihrer Schwester.**
> She apologises *to* her sister.

Prepositions and cases

In German, prepositions require certain cases. Articles, possessives or other words following a *verb + preposition* construction therefore usually take the accusative or dative case endings (**auf den Bus** *acc.*, **bei ihrer Schwester** *dat.* etc.).

List of verbs and prepositions

Here is a list of frequently used verbs and prepositions with the cases they require. Reflexive verbs are indicated with the pronoun **sich**.

an

denken an (+ *acc.*)	to think of
sich erinnern an (+ *acc.*)	to remember
sich gewöhnen an (+ *acc.*)	to get used to
glauben an (+ *acc.*)	to believe in
schreiben an (+ *acc.*)	to write to
teilnehmen an (+ *dat.*)	to take part in

auf

aufpassen auf (+ *acc.*)	to look after
antworten auf (+ *acc.*)	to answer
bestehen auf (+ *acc.*)	to insist on
sich freuen auf (+ *acc.*)	to look forward to
warten auf (+ *acc.*)	to wait for

aus

bestehen aus (+ *dat.*)	to consist of

bei

sich bedanken bei (+ *dat.*)	to say thank you to
sich bewerben bei (+ *dat.*)	to apply to
sich entschuldigen bei (+ *dat.*)	to apologise to
arbeiten bei (+ *dat.*)	to work for

für

sich bedanken für (+ *acc.*)	to thank for
sich entschuldigen für (+ *acc.*)	to apologise for
sich interessieren für (+ *acc.*)	to be interested in
sorgen für (+ *acc.*)	to care for

in

sich verlieben in (+ *acc.*)	to fall in love with

mit

anfangen mit (+ *dat.*)	to begin (with)
aufhören mit (+ *dat.*)	to stop doing something
sich beschäftigen mit (+ *dat.*)	to occupy oneself with
diskutieren mit (+ *dat.*)	to discuss with
reden mit (+ *dat.*)	to talk to

sprechen mit (+ *dat.*)	to talk to
telefonieren mit (+ *dat.*)	to talk on the phone to
vergleichen mit (+ *dat.*)	to compare to

über

sich ärgern über (+ *acc.*)	to be annoyed about
sich aufregen über (+ *acc.*)	to get upset about
sich beschweren über (+ *acc.*)	to complain about
diskutieren über (+ *acc.*)	to discuss something
sich freuen über (+ *acc.*)	to be pleased about
lachen über (+ *acc.*)	to laugh about
nachdenken über (+ *acc.*)	to think about/to reflect on
reden über (+ *acc.*)	to talk about
schreiben über (+ *acc.*)	to write about
sprechen über (+ *acc.*)	to talk about
sich streiten über (+ *acc.*)	to argue about
wissen über (+ *acc.*)	to know about

um

sich bewerben um (+ *acc.*)	to apply for
bitten um (+ *acc.*)	to ask for
sich handeln um (+ *acc.*)	to be about

von

abhängen von (+ *dat.*)	to depend on
träumen von (+ *dat.*)	to dream of
sich verabschieden von (+ *dat.*)	to take one's leave from
wissen von (+ *dat.*)	to know about

vor

sich fürchten vor (+ *dat.*)	to be afraid of

Verbs can have more than one preposition in a sentence

It is not unusual for a verb to appear with more than one preposition in a sentence. This is often the case with verbs such as **diskutieren**, **reden**, **sprechen**:

Ich rede *mit* Klaus *über* meinen Urlaub.
I talk *to* Klaus *about* my holiday.

Note that **mit** usually refers to a person, while **über** to a topic, plan, idea etc. Another verb that often appears with more than one preposition is **sich bewerben**:

> **Er bewirbt sich *bei* Ferrari *um* einen Job als Automechaniker**.
> He applies to Ferrari for a job as a car mechanic.

Prepositions can affect meaning

There are also a few verbs that change their meaning, depending on the preposition they take, such as **sich freuen + auf/über**:

> **Sie freut sich *auf* ihren Geburtstag.**
> She is *looking forward* to her birthday.

> **Sie freut sich *über* ihre Geschenke.**
> She is *pleased about* her presents.

Another example is the verb **bestehen**: **bestehen auf** 'insist on', **bestehen aus** 'consist of'.

Forming questions

Yes/no-questions

Yes/no-questions are formed by putting the verb at the beginning:

> **Glaubst du an Gott?**
> Do you believe in God?

> **Interessieren Sie sich für Sport?**
> Are you interested in sport?

With question words

More open-ended questions which contain a *verb + preposition* expression are constructed in two different ways:

- When referring to things, ideas or concepts, questions are formed by using **wo(r)** + *the relevant preposition*:

  > **denken an**   →   **Woran denkst du?**
  >   What are you thinking of?

träumen von   **Wovon hast du geträumt?**
What did you dream of?

Note that the letter **-r** is added if the preposition starts with a vowel.

- When referring to a person, the question starts with the relevant preposition, followed by the appropriate form of **wer** 'who':

denken an   → **An wen denkst du?**
Who(m) are you thinking of?

träumen von   **Von wem hast du geträumt?**
Who(m) did you dream of?

The form of **wer** depends on the case required by the preposition, hence **wen** (*acc.*) and **wem** (*dat.*).

For more details on forming questions and the various forms of **wer**, see Unit 17.

How to replace a noun or noun phrase

A noun or noun phrase which follows a *verb + preposition* construction can be replaced with:

- **da(r)** + the *relevant preposition* when referring to things, ideas or concepts; **da** corresponding to 'it'/'that'/'them' in English:

Ärgern Sie sich über *das englische Wetter*?
→ **Nein, ich ärgere mich nicht *darüber*.**

Interessierst du dich für *Fußball*?
→ **Ja, ich interessiere mich *dafür*.**

- The *relevant preposition + the personal pronoun* in the appropriate case when referring to a person:

Denkst du an *Michaela*?
→ **Nein, ich denke nicht an *sie*.** (*acc.*)

Telefonierst du mit *Frau Scior*?
→ **Ja, ich telefoniere mit *ihr*.** (*dat.*)

Commonly used expressions with darüber, daran etc.

Prepositional adverbs (**darüber**, **davon** etc.) appear in a number of expressions used in everyday spoken language. Here are a few examples:

Ich muss darüber noch nachdenken.	I still have to think about it.
Das hängt davon ab.	That depends.
Ich komme nie dazu.	I never get the time to do it/that.
Davon weiß ich nichts.	I don't know anything about that.

• For more information on prepositions, see Unit 16.

Exercise 9.1

Write down which preposition and case the verbs require and give their English meaning. Note that some verbs can take more than one preposition.

> Example: **warten** → **warten auf** + (*accusative*) – 'to wait for'
> **anfangen** → **anfangen mit** + (*dative*) – 'to begin (with)'

1 träumen, 2 aufhören, 3 sich beschäftigen, 4 sich beschweren, 5 sich bewerben, 6 denken, 7 sich erinnern, 8 sich entschuldigen, 9 sich freuen, 10 glauben, 11 sich handeln, 12 sich interessieren, 13 nachdenken, 14 teilnehmen, 15 telefonieren, 16 sich verabschieden, 17 vergleichen, 18 sich verlieben.

Exercise 9.2

Complete the following sentences by adding the appropriate prepositions and endings as shown in the example.

> Example: **Er wartet _____ d___ Bus.**
> → **Er wartet auf den Bus.**

1 Schreibst du diese E-Mail _____ dein___ Arbeitskollegin?
2 Denkst du manchmal _____ dein___ ersten Schultag?

3 Wir freuen uns schon _____ d___ Urlaub.

4 Die Kinder haben sich _____ d___ Geschenk gefreut.

5 Hast du gestern wieder _____ dein___ Bruder telefoniert?

6 Sie will _____ d___ Rauchen aufhören.

7 Hast du schon _____ dein___ Chef _____ dies___ Sache
   gesprochen?

8 Sie hat sich _____ Sony _____ ein___ Stelle als
   Fremdsprachensekretärin beworben.

Exercise 9.3

Answer each of the following questions in the negative, replacing the italicised words with **da(r)** + the relevant preposition.

> Example: **Habt ihr euch über *euer Essen* beschwert?**
> **→ Nein, wir haben uns nicht *darüber* beschwert.**

1 Interessierst du dich für *Rugby*?

2 Freust du dich auf *den Sommer*?

3 Habt ihr über *das Wetter* gesprochen?

4 Hast du dich um *die Stelle* beworben?

5 Willst du dich für *dein Benehmen* entschuldigen?

6 Hast du an *dem Seminar* teilgenommen?

Exercise 9.4

Translate the following sentences into German.

1 I am waiting for the train.

2 Lisa apologises to her brother.

3 She is pleased about the weather.

4 He is annoyed about the computer.

5 They believe in God.

6 Are you speaking to your mother? (*Use the **du** form.*)

7 Are you interested in sport? (*Use the **Sie** form.*)

8 What is she interested in?

9 That depends.

10 I don't know anything about that.

Checklist	✓
1 What do you need to be aware of when using a verb + preposition construction in German?	
2 Can you name the two prepositions that can appear with **sich freuen**?	
3 How do you form questions with a verb + preposition construction?	

UNIT TEN
The present tense

The present tense in German

The present tense in German is mainly used:

- to refer to events that are happening at the present time:

  Peter trinkt ein Bier.
  Peter is drinking beer.

- to describe habitual actions and general statements:

  Sonntags treffen wir unsere Freunde.
  On Sundays, we meet our friends.

  Die Erde dreht sich um die Sonne.
  The earth revolves around the sun.

In addition, the present tense in German often refers to the *future* when the context makes this clear:

Morgen fährt sie nach München.
Tomorrow, she will go to Munich.

There is only one present tense form in German

Note that German has only one present tense form, which corresponds to all three forms (the *simple present*, the *progressive present* and the *emphatic present*) that exist in English:

Ich arbeite = 'I work' (*simple present*)
'I am working' (*progressive present*)
'I do work' (*emphatic present*)

Formation of regular and irregular verbs

The present tense form of verbs is usually constructed by taking the stem of the infinitive and adding the appropriate personal ending.

Note that the process of changing a verb from the infinitive form into a verb with a personal ending is called *conjugation*. All verbs with a personal ending are called *finite verbs*.

In the following sections we explain the formation, patterns and spelling variations of regular and irregular verbs.

Regular verbs

Regular verbs usually add the following endings to the stem. The stem is the infinitive form of a verb without **-en** or **-n**:

		frag-en	*mach-en*	*träum-en*	*wohn-en*
ich	-e	frage	mache	träume	wohne
du	-st	fragst	machst	träumst	wohnst
Sie	-en	fragen	machen	träumen	wohnen
er/sie/es	-t	fragt	macht	träumt	wohnt
wir	-en	fragen	machen	träumen	wohnen
ihr	-t	fragt	macht	träumt	wohnt
Sie	-ten	fragen	machen	träumen	wohnen
sie	-ten	fragen	machen	träumen	wohnen

Irregular verbs

Most irregular verbs in the present tense take the same endings as regular verbs. Note that many irregular verbs require a change in their stem vowel for the **du** and **er/sie/es** forms.

		geh-en	*komm-en*	*geb-en*	*fahr-en*
ich	-e	gehe	komme	gebe	fahre
du	-st	gehst	kommst	gibst	fährst
Sie	-en	gehen	kommen	geben	fahren
er/sie/es	-t	geht	kommt	gibt	fährt

wir	-en	gehen	kommen	geben	fahren
ihr	-t	geht	kommt	gebt	fahrt
Sie	-en	gehen	kommen	geben	fahren
sie	-en	gehen	kommen	geben	fahren

For a list of irregular verbs and their stem vowel changes, see page 215.

Patterns of vowel change

There are certain patterns in the way irregular verbs change their stem vowel in the present tense. The most common ones are:

a	→	ä	fahren	du fährst, er/sie/es fährt	to drive
au	→	äu	laufen	du läufst, er/sie/es läuft	to run
e	→	i	geben	du gibst, er/sie/es gibt	to give
e	→	ie	sehen	du siehst, er/sie/es sieht	to see

Irregular verbs with different patterns

A few frequently used verbs follow an irregular pattern in the present tense: **haben** 'to have', **sein** 'to be', **werden** 'shall'/'will' or 'to become' and **wissen** 'to know':

	haben	*sein*	*werden*	*wissen*
ich	habe	bin	werde	weiß
du	hast	bist	wirst	weißt
Sie	haben	sind	werden	wissen
er/sie/es	hat	ist	wird	weiß
wir	haben	sind	werden	wissen
ihr	habt	seid	werdet	wisst
Sie	haben	sind	werden	wissen
sie	haben	sind	werden	wissen

Note that **haben**, **sein** and **werden** often function as *auxiliary verbs* as they help to form compound tenses and passive constructions.

The modal verbs **dürfen**, **können**, **müssen**, **sollen**, **wollen** and **mögen** are also quite irregular in the present tense. For an overview of all forms, see Unit 7.

Other spelling variations

- When the stem ends in either **-d**, **-t**, **-m** and **-n** an additional letter **-e** is added between the stem and the personal endings of **du**, **er/sie/es** and **ihr**.

Infinitive		Stem	Finite verb	
arbeiten	→	**arbei**t	**du arbeitest**	you work
finden		**find**	**er findet**	he finds
regnen		**regn**	**es regnet**	it rains
atmen		**atm**	**ihr atmet**	you breathe

- Verbs whose stem ends in **-s, -ß, -x, -z** only add the letter **-t** in the **du** form and not **-st**:

Infinitive		Stem	Finite verb	
reisen	→	**reis**	**du reist**	you travel
beißen		**beiß**	**du beißt**	you bite
tanzen		**tanz**	**du tanzt**	you dance

- Verbs which end in **-ern** such as **wandern** 'to hike', **ändern** 'to change' only add **-n** to the stem of the **Sie**, **wir** and plural **sie** verb forms:

ich wandere	**wir wandern**
du wanderst	**ihr wandert**
Sie wandern	**Sie wandern**
er/sie/es wandert	**sie wandern**

- In the **ich** form verbs ending in **-eln** such as **sammeln** 'to collect', **lächeln** 'to smile' drop the letter **-e** before the **-l**:

  Ich handle mit Computersoftware.
  I trade in computer software.

  Ich sammle alte Autos.
  I collect old cars.

- For a list of modal verbs in the present tense, see Unit 7.
- For more information on separable verbs in the present tense, see Unit 8.
- For the use of the present tense referring to the future, see Unit 14.

Exercise 10.1

Indicate which of the irregular verbs in the following list change their stem vowel in the present tense by marking them with a ✓ and put a ✗ next to those that do not. You can use the list on page 215 to help you. The first two have been done for you.

1	fahren ✓	7	gefallen ✓	13	essen ✓	19	sprechen ✓
2	bleiben ✗	8	sitzen ✗	14	schwimmen ✓	20	waschen ✗
3	sehen ✓	9	laufen ✓	15	trinken ✗	21	schlafen ✓
4	fangen ✗	10	kennen ✗	16	vergessen ✓	22	helfen
5	geben ✓	11	tragen ✓	17	werden ✓	23	gehen ✗
6	bringen ✗	12	kommen ✗	18	treffen ✓	24	empfehlen ✓

Exercise 10.2

Now write out the **ich, du** and **er/sie/es** form of all verbs with a stem vowel change from Exercise 10.1.

Exercise 10.3

Write out the full present tense forms (**ich, du, Sie, er/sie/es, wir, ihr, Sie, sie**) of the following verbs:

1 arbeiten; 2 finden; 3 rechnen; 4 grüßen; 5 tanzen; 6 sammeln; 7 behandeln; 8 ändern.

Exercise 10.4

Translate the sentences below into German.

1 She works in Bern.
2 Yes, he does work today!
3 She is seeing a film.
4 You are driving too fast. (*Use the du, Sie and ihr forms.*)
5 She runs slowly.
6 He finds the keys.
7 I collect old postcards.
8 Do you like dancing? (*Use the du, Sie and ihr forms.*)
9 Are you from New York? (*Use the du, Sie and ihr forms.*)
10 You know how expensive life in London is. (*Use the du, Sie and ihr forms.*)

Checklist	✓
1 Can you list all personal endings of the regular verb **hören** in the present tense?	höre hörst hört hören hören
2 Do you remember four patterns of vowel changes with irregular verbs?	e = i a = ä
3 Which four frequently used verbs have a different pattern of change?	haben werden sein wissen
4 What happens to verbs ending in **-eln** and **-ern** in their present tense forms?	
5 Apart from the present, to what other time can the present tense also refer in German?	

UNIT ELEVEN
The present perfect tense

Usage in English

In English, the present perfect tense is used for past events that are linked to the present. This stands in contrast to the simple past tense, which refers to actions that were completed in the past:

present perfect	They have not arrived yet.
simple past	They arrived last week.

The present perfect tense in German

In German, it is not relevant whether a past event refers to the present in some way or if the action was completed in the past. Instead, the main difference in usage is based on the following:

- the present perfect is generally used when *speaking* about the past, irrespective of how long ago an event occurred; and
- the simple past is mainly used in the *written* language.

Formation – the main principles

The present perfect is a compound tense, which is constructed with the appropriate form of **haben** or **sein** + the *past participle* of the relevant verb. There are three main patterns:

- *Regular* verbs usually take **haben** and form the past participle by adding **ge-** + **t** to the stem:

  Wie hast du das gemacht?
  How did you do that?

- *Irregular* verbs also usually use **haben**. The past participles tend to end in **-en** rather than **-t** and often undergo a vowel change:

  Er hat Kaffee getrunken.
  He drank coffee.

- Verbs referring to *movement* or a *change of state* take **sein**:

  Sie ist mit KLM geflogen.
  She flew with KLM.

Here are the forms in more detail.

Regular verbs

Formation

The present perfect tense of most regular verbs is constructed by using the present tense of **haben** + the *past participle* of the relevant verb.

The past participle is formed with the *stem* of the verb, which is the infinitive without **-(e)n**. The prefix **ge-** is then added at the beginning and the letter **-t** at the end:

Infinitive	*Stem*	*Past participle*	
hören →	**hör**	*ge* + **hör** + *t*	listened, heard
sagen	**sag**	*ge* + **sag** + *t*	said
lächeln	**lächel**	*ge* + **lächel** + *t*	smiled

Irregular verbs

Adding ge- + -en to the stem

The past participle of most irregular verbs are formed by putting **ge-** in front of the stem and **-en** at the end:

Infinitive	*Stem*	*Past participle*	
lesen →	**les**	*ge* + **les** + **en**	read
sehen	**seh**	*ge* + **seh** + **en**	seen
waschen	**wasch**	*ge* + **wasch** + **en**	washed

Stem vowel change

Many irregular verbs have a stem vowel change:

Infinitive	Past participle	
fi*n*den →	**gef*u*nden**	found
h*e*lfen	**geh*o*lfen**	helped
schr*ei*ben	**geschr*ie*ben**	written
fl*ie*gen	**gefl*o*gen**	flown

Note that many German irregular verbs tend to be irregular in English. A good way to learn irregular verb forms is to work with a list of verbs, which you can find at the end of this book and in most dictionaries.

There are also some patterns of stem vowel changes. For more information, see page 93.

Mixed verbs – stem vowel change, but ending in -t

There are verbs called mixed verbs which combine the characteristics of regular and irregular verbs as they *change their stem vowel* and *add* **-t** when forming the past participle. Here are some examples:

Infinitive	Past participle	
brennen →	**gebrannt**	burned
bringen	**gebracht**	brought
denken	**gedacht**	thought
kennen	**gekannt**	known
nennen	**genannt**	named
wissen	**gewusst**	known

Verbs taking sein

A number of verbs in German form their present perfect tense with the present tense of **sein** + *past participle*. They can be divided into the following groups:

Verbs indicating movement from one location to another

This group contains commonly used *irregular verbs* such as **gehen** 'to go', **fahren** 'to go (by vehicle)', **kommen** 'to come', **ankommen** 'to arrive', **laufen** 'to run':

Ich bin ins Kino gegangen.
I have gone/went to the cinema.

Seid ihr mit dem Auto gefahren?
Did you go by car?

Jörg ist den ganzen Weg gelaufen.
Jörg has run/ran the whole way.

There are also a few *regular verbs* indicating movement such as **joggen** 'to jog', **reisen** 'to travel', **segeln** 'to sail' and **wandern** 'to hike' which require **sein**:

Robert ist letztes Jahr durch Asien gereist.
Robert travelled through Asia last year.

Sie sind in den Alpen gewandert.
They went hiking in the Alps.

Verbs expressing a change of state

Another group of verbs indicates a process or a change of state. They include **aufstehen** 'to get up', **einschlafen** 'to fall asleep', **sterben** 'to die', **wachsen** 'to grow', **werden** 'to become':

Er ist Ingenieur geworden.
He has become/became an engineer.

Du bist aber gewachsen!
How you have grown!

Wir sind sehr früh eingeschlafen.
We fell asleep very early.

Other verbs – bleiben, passieren, sein

There are three other verbs which also take **sein** to form the present perfect: **bleiben** 'to stay', **passieren** 'to happen' and **sein** 'to be':

Wir sind nur eine Woche geblieben.
We only stayed for a week.

Was ist denn passiert?
What (has) happened?

Er ist noch nie in Berlin gewesen.
He has never been to Berlin.

Usage with haben

Sometimes, the verbs **fahren** and **fliegen** form their present perfect with **haben** when the focus is on the driver or pilot. However, this usage is quite rare:

Er *hat* das Auto selbst gefahren.
He drove the car himself.

Sie *hat* den Hubschrauber geflogen.
She flew the helicopter (herself).

Other points to watch out for

Some past participles don't start with ge-

Note that some of the following verbs form their past participles without adding **ge-**:

- Verbs ending in **-ieren**, such as **buchstabieren** 'to spell', **probieren** 'to try', **reagieren** 'to react', **studieren** 'to study', **telefonieren** 'to telephone':

    Sie hat schnell reagiert.
    She (has) reacted quickly.

    Wir haben in Marseille studiert.
    We studied in Marseille.

- Verbs with the inseparable prefixes **be-**, **emp-**, **ent-**, **er-**, **ge-**, **miss-**, **ver-**, **zer-**:

    Ich habe mit Kreditkarte bezahlt.
    I (have) paid by credit card.

    Der Kellner hat mir die Suppe empfohlen.
    The waiter (has) recommended the soup to me.

For more information on verbs with inseparable prefixes, see Unit 9.

Separable verbs

Separable verbs form their past participles by placing '**ge**' between the separable prefix and the main verb: **ankommen** → **an*ge*kommen**, **fernsehen** → **fern*ge*sehen**:

Wann seid ihr angekommen?
When did you arrive?

Hast du gestern ferngesehen?
Did you watch TV last night?

Word order

In a *main clause* the relevant form of **haben** or **sein** is the second element and the past participle moves to the end:

Er *hat* die Tür *aufgemacht*.
He (has) opened the door.

Wir *sind* nur eine Woche *geblieben*.
We only stayed for a week.

In *subordinate clauses*, the appropriate form of **haben** or **sein** is usually placed in the last position. It is preceded by the past participle:

Es stimmt, dass er früher in Tirol gelebt *hat*.
It is true that he used to live in the Tyrol.

Ich denke, dass sie mit dem Auto gefahren *sind*.
I think that they went by car.

Using the simple past instead of the present perfect

Although the present perfect is normally used when talking about past events, it is quite common to use the *simple past tense* of *modal verbs* in spoken German:

Ich konnte gestern nicht kommen.
I couldn't come yesterday.

Was wolltest du eigentlich kaufen?
What did you actually want to buy?

Note also that the present perfect of **haben** and **sein** is often replaced with the *simple past* forms:

Ich habe Urlaub gehabt.   →   **Ich hatte Urlaub.**
Ich bin im Kino gewesen.   →   **Ich war im Kino.**

- For more details on modal verbs in the simple past tense, see Unit 7.
- For all forms of **haben** and **sein** in the simple past tense, see Unit 12.
- For more information on irregular verb changes, see Unit 12.
- For a list of irregular verbs, see pages 215–17.

Exercise 11.1

Which of the following verbs are *regular, irregular* and so-called *mixed* verbs? Put each one in the appropriate column. The first one has been done for you.

1 schreiben	7 passieren	13 rennen	19 wachsen
2 tanzen	8 fahren	14 bringen	20 wissen
3 fliegen	9 machen	15 hören	21 kennen
4 reservieren	10 trinken	16 besuchen	22 kommen
5 stellen	11 helfen	17 reisen	23 nennen
6 denken	12 bleiben	18 sein	24 verstehen

Regular verbs	Irregular verbs	Mixed verbs
kommen stellen tanzen trinken hören reservieren machen	schreiben- helfen fliegen gahren sein wachsen reisen passieren besuchen	bringen denken wissen rennen bleiben kennen nennen passieren verstehen

Exercise 11.2

Write down the past participle forms of all verbs in Exercise 11.1.

Example: **schreiben** → *geschrieben*

Nine of these verbs require **sein** to form the present perfect. Can you identify them?

Exercise 11.3

Follow the two examples and put the sentences below into the present perfect tense.

Examples: **Ich gehe oft spät ins Bett.**
→ **Früher *bin* ich nie spät ins Bett *gegangen*.**

Er hat jetzt kurze Haare.
→ **Früher *hat* er nie kurze Haare *gehabt*.**

1   Sie liest jetzt immer die Zeitung.
2   Er hört klassische Musik.
3   Jetzt fahren wir mit dem Bus.
4   Du schreibst meistens E-Mails.
5   Wir gehen oft aus.
6   Sie kaufen im Supermarkt ein.
7   Er läuft jetzt jeden Morgen.
8   Sie bleiben jetzt immer zu Hause.

Exercise 11.4

Translate the following sentences into German, using the present perfect tense.

1   Have you eaten something?
    (*Use the **Sie** form.*)
2   What did he say?
3   She studied in Germany.
4   I flew with Air Berlin.
5   We only stayed three days.
6   They never used to watch TV.
7   What's happened?
8   Marc phoned his mother.
9   The tree has hardly grown.
10   He became a journalist.

Checklist	✓
1 When is the present perfect tense normally used in German?	
2 How do you form the past participle for regular and irregular verbs?	
3 Can you explain what a mixed verb is and give an example?	
4 When do you form the present perfect tense with **sein**?	
5 How do separable verbs form their past participles?	

UNIT TWELVE

The simple past tense

Usage in German

The simple past tense in German is usually used in the written language, especially in articles, reports, novels and CVs.

Der Bundeskanzler eröffnete das neue Messezentrum.
The Federal Chancellor opened the new trade fair centre.

Mit 19 Jahren begann ich mein Jurastudium.
When I was 19, I began to study law.

In modern German grammar terms the simple past tense is called *Präteritum* 'preterite'. However, it is often still referred to as *Imperfekt* 'imperfect'.

Regular verbs

Formation

Regular verbs do not change the vowel in their stem. The simple past tense is formed by adding the appropriate personal endings:

		frag-en	*mach-en*	*träum-en*	*wohn-en*
ich	-te	frag*te*	mach*te*	*träumte*	wohn*te*
du	-test	frag*test*	mach*test*	träumte	wohntest
~~Sie~~	~~-ten~~	~~fragten~~	~~machten~~	~~träumten~~	~~wohnten~~
er/sie/es	-te	frag*te*	mach*te*	träumte	wohn*te*
wir	-ten	frag*ten*	mach*ten*	träumten	wohn*ten*
ihr	-tet	frag*tet*	mach*tet*	träumtet	wohn*tet*
~~Sie~~	~~-ten~~	~~fragten~~	~~machten~~	~~träumten~~	~~wohnten~~
sie	-ten	frag*ten*	mach*ten*	träumten	wohn*ten*

Note that the above endings are similar to the present tense, with the exception of **er/sie/es**, which end in **-e**:

Ich machte meine Hausaufgaben immer im letzten Moment.
I always did my homework at the last moment.

Er wohnte drei Jahre in der Schweiz.
He lived for three years in Switzerland.

Variations in personal endings

With regular verbs whose stems end in **-d,-m**, **-n** or **-t** such as **arbeiten** 'to work', an extra **-e** is added:

ich arbeitete	**wir arbeiteten**
du arbeitetest	**ihr arbeitetet**
~~Sie arbeiten~~	~~Sie arbeiten~~
er/sie/es arbeitete	**sie arbeiteten**

Other verbs following this pattern include **atmen** 'to breathe', **begegnen** 'to meet', **beobachten** 'to observe', **öffnen** 'to open', **rechnen** 'to calculate', **reden** 'to talk', **retten** 'to rescue', **warten** 'to wait'.

Er redete die ganze Zeit, während wir arbeiteten.
He talked continuously while we were working.

Irregular verbs

Irregular verbs either change their stem vowel (**bleiben → blieb**, **geben → gab**), or sometimes their whole stem (**gehen → ging**). The following personal endings are added to the modified stem:

		bleib-en	*geb-en*	*geh-en*	*sing-en*
		blieb	*gab*	*ging*	*sang*
ich	–	blieb	gab	ging	sang
du	-st	bliebst	gabst	gingst	sangst
~~Sie~~	~~-en~~	~~blieben~~	~~gaben~~	~~gingen~~	~~sangen~~
er/sie/es	–	blieb	gab	ging	sang
wir	-en	blieben	gaben	gingen	sangen
ihr	-t	bliebt	gabt	gingt	sangt
~~Sie~~	~~-en~~	~~blieben~~	~~gaben~~	~~gingen~~	~~sangen~~
sie	-en	blieben	gaben	gingen	sangen

Note that the **ich** and **er/sie/es** forms have *no* endings.

Ich *blieb* für eine Woche in Toronto.
I stayed in Toronto for one week.

Abends *ging* er noch in eine Bar.
In the evening, he went on to a bar.

Variations in personal endings

When the stem of an irregular verb in the simple past ends in **-d**,
-s/ss/ß or **-t**, an additional **-e** is added to the **du** form and sometimes also
the **ihr** form:

finden	→	**fand**	**du fandest**	**ihr fandet**
beißen		**biss**	**du bissest**	**ihr bisset**
sitzen		**saß**	**du saßest**	**ihr saßt**
reiten		**ritt**	**du rittest**	**ihr rittet**
schneiden		**schnitt**	**du schnittest**	**ihr schnittet**

Note that these **du** and **ihr** forms are often replaced with the present
perfect tense:

Fandest du dein Telefonbuch?
→ **Hast du dein Telefonbuch gefunden?**

Saßet ihr in der ersten Reihe?
→ **Habt ihr in der ersten Reihe gesessen?**

Mixed verbs and modal verbs

Mixed verbs

There are verbs called *mixed verbs* that have a stem vowel change but
take the endings of regular verbs. The most common of these are:

Infinitive		*Simple past*	
brennen	→	**brannte**	burned
bringen		**brachte**	brought
denken		**dachte**	thought
kennen		**kannte**	knew
nennen		**nannte**	named
rennen		**rannte**	ran
wissen		**wusste**	knew

Ich kannte seine Eltern.
I knew his parents.

Er rannte sehr schnell nach Hause.
He ran home very fast.

Sie wussten nicht, dass es schon so spät war.
They didn't know that it was so late.

Modal verbs

Modal verbs form their simple past tense in a similar way to mixed verbs. They change their stem vowel but use regular verb endings for the simple past endings.

As an example, here are all simple past tense forms of **müssen** 'must, to have to':

ich musste, du musstest, Sie mussten, er/sie/es musste, wir mussten, ihr musstet, Sie mussten, sie mussten.

For a list of all modal verbs in the simple past tense, see Unit 7.

Irregular verbs with different patterns –
haben, sein **and** werden

Here are all forms of the frequently used verbs **haben** 'to have', **sein** 'to be' and **werden** 'will'/'shall', 'to become':

	haben	*sein*	*werden*
ich	hatte	war	wurde
du	hattest	warst	wurdest
Sie	hatten	waren	wurden
er/sie/es	hatte	war	wurde
wir	hatten	waren	wurden
ihr	hattet	wart	wurdet
Sie	hatten	waren	wurden
sie	hatten	waren	wurden

Patterns of stem vowel changes

Many irregular and mixed verbs follow certain patterns when changing their stems in the simple past and the present perfect tenses. The five most common patterns are:

	Infinitive	*Simple past*	*Past participle*	
ei – i – i	leiden	litt	gelitten	to suffer
	reiten	ritt	geritten	to ride
	schneiden	schnitt	geschnitten	to cut
ei – ie – ie	bleiben	blieb	geblieben	to stay
	scheinen	schien	geschienen	to seem, to shine
	schreiben	schrieb	geschrieben	to write
i – a – u	finden	fand	gefunden	to find
	singen	sang	gesungen	to sing
	trinken	trank	getrunken	to drink
ie – o – o	fliegen	flog	geflogen	to fly
	schließen	schloss	geschlossen	to close
	verlieren	verlor	verloren	to lose
e – a – o	brechen	brach	gebrochen	to break
	sprechen	sprach	gesprochen	to speak
	sterben	starb	gestorben	to die

- For more details on modal verbs in the simple past tense, see Unit 7.
- For information on separable verbs in the simple past tense, see Unit 8.
- For a list of irregular verbs, see pages 215–17.

Exercise 12.1

Write out the full simple past tense of the following verbs for all persons: **ich**, **du**, **Sie**, **er/sie/es**, **wir ihr**, **Sie**, **sie**.

1 wohnen; 2 fragen; 3 arbeiten; 4 reden; 5 kommen; 6 schreiben; 7 nennen; 8 gehen.

Exercise 12.2

Fill in the gaps below by using the simple past form of the verb before the comma.

> Example: **Er wollte nicht schlafen, aber dann _____ er doch.**
> → **Er wollte nicht schlafen, aber dann *schlief* er doch.**

1 Ich wollte nicht lange bleiben, aber dann _blieb_ ich bis Mitternacht.
2 Wir wollten nichts trinken, aber dann _tranken_ wir doch etwas.
3 Sie mussten nach Berlin fliegen, aber dann _flogen_ sie nach Paris.
4 Placido Domingo sollte erst nicht singen, aber dann _sang_ er doch.
5 Sie wollte nicht telefonieren, aber dann _telefonierte_ sich doch.
6 Es sollte nicht regnen, aber dann _regnete_ es den ganzen Nachmittag.

Exercise 12.3

Here is a short version of the fairy tale Hansel and Gretel by the Grimm brothers. Fill in each gap by using the appropriate simple past form of the verb or verbs in brackets. The first one has been done for you.

1 Hänsel und Gretel *gingen* in den Wald. (gehen)
2 Die Kinder _kamen_ an ein kleines Häuschen. (kommen)
3 Vor dem Häuschen _stand_ eine Hexe. (stehen)
4 Die Hexe _gab_ ihnen Pfefferkuchen. (geben)
5 Hänsel und Gretel _waren_ sehr müde und _gingen_ ins Bett. (sein, gehen)
6 Am nächsten Morgen _musste_ Gretel früh aufstehen und arbeiten. (müssen)
7 Die Hexe _wollte_ Hänsel im Ofen braten und essen. (wollen)
8 Die Kinder _hatten_ einen Plan, um der Hexe zu entfliehen. (haben)
9 Sie _stießen_ die Hexe in den Ofen. (stoßen)
10 Dann _liefen_ sie nach Hause. (laufen)

Exercise 12.4

Translate the following sentences into German by using the simple past tense.

1 I made a coffee.
2 We stayed until midnight.
3 They forgot his address.

4 She took her bag and drove into town.
5 Last week I flew to Vienna.
6 The children ran to school.
7 They worked in the garden.
8 I read the book.
9 It rained the whole day.
10 I didn't know that it was so late.

Checklist	✓
1 What is the simple past tense called in German?	
2 Can you list the endings for regular verbs in the simple past tense?	
3 How do most irregular verbs change?	
4 Do you know all the simple past tense forms of **haben**, **sein** and **werden**?	
5 Which pattern of stem vowel changes would you apply for **finden** or **trinken** in the present perfect and simple past tenses?	

UNIT THIRTEEN
The past perfect tense

What is the past perfect tense?

The past perfect tense, also called the pluperfect tense, is one of the three past tenses in German. It is used when speaking or writing about the past to refer to events that happened earlier:

> **Gestern traf ich Karl. Wir *hatten* uns seit 20 Jahren nicht *gesehen*.**
> Yesterday, I met Karl. We hadn't seen each other for 20 years.

Formation of the past perfect

The past perfect tense is a compound tense. It is formed with the *simple past tense* of **haben** or **sein** + *the past participle* of the main verb:

> **Sie aß sehr wenig, denn sie *hatte* schon zu Mittag *gegessen*.**
> She ate very little because she had eaten lunch already.

> **Er wollte Spanish lernen, nachdem er durch Mexiko *gereist war*.**
> He wanted to learn Spanish after he had travelled through Mexico.

Past perfect with haben

The past perfect for most verbs is formed by using the appropriate *simple past* form of **haben** + *the past participle* of the relevant verb. This applies to regular and irregular verbs that take **haben** in the *present perfect tense*:

		kauf-en	*les-en*	*seh-en*
ich	hatte	gekauft	gelesen	gesehen
du	hattest	gekauft	gelesen	gesehen
Sie	hatten	gekauft	gelesen	gesehen
er/sie/es	hatte	gekauft	gelesen	gesehen
wir	hatten	gekauft	gelesen	gesehen
ihr	hattet	gekauft	gelesen	gesehen
Sie	hatten	gekauft	gelesen	gesehen
sie	hatten	gekauft	gelesen	gesehen

Nachdem er einen Computer *gekauft hatte*, surfte er im Internet.
After having bought a computer, he surfed the Internet.

Wir *hatten* zum Glück Goethes Faust *gelesen* und konnten die Fragen beantworten.
Fortunately, we had read Goethe's Faust and could answer the questions.

For more information on verbs taking **haben** and how to form the past participle, see Unit 11.

Past perfect with sein

Some regular and irregular verbs take the *simple past* tense of **sein** + *past participle* when forming the past perfect tense:

		reis-en	*geh-en*	*einschlaf-en*
ich	war	gereist	gegangen	eingeschlafen
du	warst	gereist	gegangen	eingeschlafen
Sie	waren	gereist	gegangen	eingeschlafen
er/sie/es	war	gereist	gegangen	eingeschlafen
wir	waren	gereist	gegangen	eingeschlafen
ihr	wart	gereist	gegangen	eingeschlafen
Sie	waren	gereist	gegangen	eingeschlafen
sie	waren	gereist	gegangen	eingeschlafen

Ich wusste nicht, dass er nach Deutschland gereist war.
I didn't know that he had travelled to Germany.

Nachdem die Eltern nach Hause gegangen *waren*, feierten die jungen Leute weiter.
After their parents had gone home, the youngsters continued to party.

For more information on verbs taking **sein**, see Unit 11.

The past perfect in main and subordinate clauses

Main clauses

In main clauses, the simple past of **haben** or **sein** is the second element and the past participle is placed at the end:

Wir *hatten* uns seit der Schulzeit nicht mehr *gesehen*.
We hadn't seen each other since we left school.

Subordinate clauses

In *subordinate clauses*, the relevant form of **haben** or **sein** moves to the end of the clause, preceded by the *past participle*:

Ich öffnete die Tür, nachdem ich den Schlüssel *gefunden hatte*.
I opened the door after I had found the key.

Ich machte ihm Kaffee, nachdem er *angekommen war*.
I made him coffee after he had arrived.

Note that subordinate clauses in the past perfect tense are often introduced by the conjunction **nachdem** 'after'.

Usage with other past tenses

When the past perfect tense is used in a subordinate clause, the main clause connected to it can either be in the *present perfect* or *simple past* tense:

Present perfect   **Ich habe die Tür geöffnet, nachdem ich den Schlüssel gefunden hatte.**

Simple past   **Ich öffnete die Tür, nachdem ich den Schlüssel gefunden hatte.**

Present perfect **Ich habe meinen Kaffee getrunken, nachdem ich abgewaschen hatte.**
Simple past   **Ich trank meinen Kaffee, nachdem ich abgewaschen hatte.**

Alternative to the past perfect

In German, the past perfect tense is often substituted with the present perfect, especially in spoken German:

Er sprach besser Englisch, nachdem er ein Jahr in York gelebt hatte.
→ Er sprach besser Englisch, nachdem er ein Jahr in York gelebt hat.

However, in order to clarify the sequence of past events, it is sometimes necessary to use the past perfect even in colloquial speech:

Nachdem wir alle Zutaten gekauft hatten, kochten wir das Mittagessen.
After we had bought all the ingredients, we cooked lunch.

- For more information on forming the past participle, see Unit 11.

Exercise 13.1

Complete the following sentences with the appropriate forms of **haben** or **sein**.

Example: **Er hatte einen schönen Teint, weil er seinen Urlaub auf Mallorca verbracht _____ .**
→ Er hatte einen schönen Teint, weil er seinen Urlaub auf Mallorca verbracht *hatte*.

1 Sie war sehr müde, weil sie sieben Stunden lang ohne Pause gearbeitet _hatte_ .
2 Er sagte mir, wohin er letztes Jahr gefahren *~~hatte~~ war* .
3 Wir mussten uns beeilen, denn wir _waren_ zu spät aufgestanden.

4 Ich konnte nicht kommen, da ich den Zug verpasst _hatte_ .
5 Er kam um Mitternacht nach Hause, weil er noch ins Restaurant
   gegangen _war_ .
6 Die Leute waren überrascht, denn so etwas _war_ noch nie passiert.

Exercise 13.2

Complete the following sentences in the past perfect tense, starting with
davor 'before that'.

Example:

Kurt lebte lange Zeit in Rom. Davor _____ er in Bari _____ .
→ **Kurt lebte lange Zeit in Rom. Davor _hatte_ er in Bari _gelebt_.**

1 Ich trank nur noch Mineralwasser. Davor _hatte_ ich meistens Bier
   getrunken .
2 Peter konnte nicht viel essen. Davor _hatte_ er schon ein Würstchen
   gegessen .
3 Sie trug gestern eine Jeans. Davor _hatte_ sie nie Jeans _getragen_ .
4 Wir gingen dann noch in eine Bar. Davor _waren_ wir ins Kino
   gegangen .

Exercise 13.3

Convert the following sentences by using **nachdem** as shown in the
example:

Example: **Zuerst ging ich einkaufen. Dann las ich die Zeitung.**
          → **Nachdem ich einkaufen gegangen war, las ich die**
          Zeitung.

1 Ich kochte das Mittagessen. Dann ging ich im Park spazieren.
2 Ich kam nach Hause. Dann rief ich meinen Bruder an.
3 Ich schrieb eine E-Mail. Dann traf ich ein paar Freunde in der
   Kneipe.
4 Ich sah die Spätnachrichten im Fernsehen. Dann ging ich ins Bett.

Exercise 13.4

Translate the sentences below into German, using the past perfect tense.

1 We hadn't seen each other for 10 years.
2 Before that I had lived in Hamburg.
3 Before that he had been a doctor.
4 She couldn't come because she had missed the train.
5 I didn't know that you had been to Austria. (*Use the **du** form.*)
6 He wanted to read the book after he had seen the film.
7 They spoke better Spanish after they had lived in Madrid.
8 After she had washed the car she drove into town.

Checklist	✓
1 When is the past perfect tense used?	
2 How do you form the past perfect?	
3 Which conjunction often introduces a subordinate clause in the past perfect tense?	
4 How can the past perfect tense often be substituted?	

UNIT FOURTEEN
The future tense

Referring to the future in German

The *future tense* in German is formed with the verb **werden**:

Wirst du in Zukunft öfters im Ausland arbeiten?
Will you be working abroad more often in future?

Wir werden uns wahrscheinlich verspäten.
We will probably be delayed.

Note that there is also another less frequently used future tense in German, the *future perfect tense*. For more details see pages 104–5.

Formation of the future tense

The future tense is constructed with the present tense form of the auxiliary verb **werden** + *the infinitive* of the relevant verb:

Ich *werde* den Zug *versäumen*.	I shall/will miss the train.
Du *wirst* dich morgen besser *fühlen*.	You will feel better tomorrow.
***Werden* Sie zur Party *kommen*?**	Will you come to the party?
Er *wird* das gleich *erledigen*.	He will deal with it at once.
Wir *werden* heute *anfangen*.	We shall/will start today.
Ihr *werdet* alles *erfahren*.	You will find out everything.
***Werden* Sie tanzen *gehen*?**	Will you go dancing?
Was *werden* sie *sagen*?	What will they say?

Note that **werden** is an irregular verb and changes its stem vowel in the **du** and **er/sie/es** forms.

Usage and functions

The future tense is used less frequently in German than in English. If the context makes the reference to the future clear the present tense is normally used instead. However, the future tense still occurs in the following instances:

- When the reference to the future is not clear:

    Tim wird wieder in Köln wohnen.
    Tim will be living in Cologne again.

    The alternative in the present tense **Tim wohnt wieder in Köln** would be understood as 'Thomas is now living again in Cologne'.

- When stating intentions or to emphasise a point:

    Ich werde nie wieder den Bus nehmen!
    Never again will I take the bus!

    Ich werde die Miete morgen bezahlen.
    I will pay the rent tomorrow.

- To make predictions and to convey the meaning of probability or assumption, often in conjunction with **bestimmt** 'surely', **wahrscheinlich** 'probably', **möglicherweise** 'possibly', **vielleicht** 'maybe', **wohl** 'probably':

    Morgen wird es regnen.
    It's going to rain tomorrow.

    Es wird bestimmt nicht lange dauern.
    Surely it won't take long.

    Das wird wahrscheinlich funktionieren.
    That will probably work.

    Ich werde vielleicht kommen.
    Maybe I will come.

Using the present tense to refer to the future

In German, the present tense – rather than the future tense – is normally used to refer to the future, especially when this is clearly indicated by an expression of time:

Ich komme *gleich* wieder.
I'll be right back.

In zwei Tagen **bin ich in New York.**
In two days, I'll be in New York.

Das Konzert findet *morgen* **statt.**
The concert will take place tomorrow.

Sie heiraten *nächstes Jahr.*
They will get married next year.

Frequently used words or expressions to indicate the future include: **bald** 'soon', **demnächst** 'soon'/'before long', **gleich** 'right away', **in zwei Tagen/ Wochen/Monaten** etc. 'in two days/weeks/months' etc., **morgen** 'tomorrow', **nächstes Wochenende/nächste Woche** etc. 'next weekend'/'next week' etc.

Difference between 'will' and 'want to' in German

Be careful not to confuse the English 'will' indicating the future, with the German modal **will** meaning 'want/s to' in German:

Ich *will* **jetzt essen.**
I *want to* eat now.

Ich *werde* **weniger essen.**
I *will* eat less.

The future perfect

Formation

The future perfect is used to refer to events that will be completed in the future. It is formed with the present tense form of **werden** + *past participle* of the main verb + the *infinitive forms* of **haben** or **sein**:

In zwei Jahren wirst du das Auto abbezahlt haben.
In two years you will have paid for the car.

Er wird wahrscheinlich morgen noch nicht abgereist sein.
He will probably not have left by tomorrow.

Usage

The future perfect tense is rarely used in contemporary German and is usually replaced by the shorter construction of the appropriate present tense form of **haben** or **sein** + *past participle*:

In zwei Jahren wirst du das Auto abbezahlt haben.
→ **In zwei Jahren hast du das Auto abbezahlt.**

Er wird wahrscheinlich morgen noch nicht abgereist sein.
→ **Er ist wahrscheinlich morgen noch nicht abgereist.**

Exercise 14.1

Write out the present tense forms of **werden** for all persons: **ich, du, Sie, er/sie/es, wir, ihr, Sie, sie.**

[handwritten: Ich werde / du/Sie wirst / er/sie/es/man wird / wir werden / ihr werdet / sie/sie werden]

Exercise 14.2

Put more emphasis on the following statements by using the future tense with **werden**.

Example: **Morgen gehen wir ins Kino.**
→ **Morgen werden wir ins Kino gehen.**

1 Nächste Woche kaufen sie ein neues Auto. *[handwritten: Nächste Woche werden sie ein neues Auto kaufen]*
2 Im April besuche ich dich. *[handwritten: Im April werde ich dich besuchen]*
3 Er verkauft sein Haus. *[handwritten: Er wird sein Haus verkaufen]*
4 Ihr geht am Nachmittag einkaufen. *[handwritten: Ihr werdet am Nachmittag einkaufen gehen]*
5 Ich sehe weniger fern. *[handwritten: Ich werde weniger fern sehen]*
6 Am Wochenende arbeite ich. *[handwritten: Am Wochenende werde ich arbeiten]*
7 In drei Tagen fahren wir in Urlaub. *[handwritten: In drei Tagen werden wir in Urlaub fahren]*
8 Der Zug kommt bestimmt bald. *[handwritten: Der Zug wird bestimmt bald kommen]*

Exercise 14.3

Transform the following sentences from the *future perfect* into an alternative construction as shown in the example:

Example: **Im August wirst du sicher das Examen bestanden haben.**
→ **Im August *hast* du sicher das Examen *bestanden*.**

1   Nächstes Wochenende wirst du deinen Kurs beendet haben.
2   Morgen um diese Zeit wirst du schon in Berlin angekommen sein.
3   Er wird wohl schon wieder krank gewesen sein.
4   Bis nächsten Freitag werden sie unseren Brief erhalten haben.

3. Er ist wohl schon wieder krank gewesen
4. Bis nächsten Freitag haben sie unseren Brief erhalten

Exercise 14.4

Translate the following sentences into German, using the future tense with
werden.

1   I'll call you tomorrow. (*Use the **du** form.*)
2   She'll be working until 6 o'clock.
3   We'll miss the bus.
4   What are you doing this evening? (*Use the **du**, **Sie** and **ihr** forms.*)
5   Will you come to London next summer? (*Use the **du**, **Sie** and **ihr**
    forms.*)
6   It's going to rain tomorrow.
7   It won't take long.
8   He'll probably be at home.
9   She will surely come to the party.
10 In six months I will have paid for the new Audi.

Checklist	*(present) + infinitive* *werden*	✓
1 How do you form the future tense in German?		
2 Can you name three instances in which the future tense is normally used in German? *predictions, emphasis, ambiguity*		
3 How do you form the future perfect? *werden, P.P. (pres) (inf) haben/sein*		
4 Can you give the different meanings of **ich will** and **ich werde**? *(want) (will)*		

UNIT FIFTEEN
Adjectives and adverbs

Use of adjectives

Adjectives provide more information about nouns:

Dieses Handy ist *teuer.*
This mobile phone is expensive.

Sie ist eine *interessante* **Frau.**
She is an interesting woman.

Adjectives can either appear after the noun (**Dieses Handy ist teuer**) or directly in front of the noun they describe (**eine interessante Frau**).

Adjectives after nouns – do not take endings

Adjectives do not change when they appear after the noun they describe. This is often the case in connection with the verbs **sein** 'to be' and **werden** 'to become':

Michael ist immer schon ein bisschen *komisch* **gewesen.**
Michael has always been a bit funny.

Ihr Gesicht wurde *dunkelrot.*
Her face turned purple.

Adjectives before nouns – take endings

An adjective preceding a noun normally requires an ending. The patterns of endings depend on whether the adjective appears:

- with *no* article
- with an *indefinite* article *or*
- with a *definite* article.

All three patterns are explained in the following sections.

Adjectives with no article

Here is an overview of adjective endings with no preceding article:

	Masculine	*Feminine*	*Neuter*	*Plural*
Nom.	deutscher Wein	deutsche Musik	deutsches Bier	deutsche Touristen
Acc.	deutschen Wein	deutsche Musik	deutsches Bier	deutsche Touristen
Dat.	deutschem Wein	deutscher Musik	deutschem Bier	deutschen Touristen
Gen.	deutschen Wein(e)s	deutscher Musik	deutschen Bier(e)s	deutscher Touristen

Note that in the absence of an article, the adjectives function as 'markers' for the noun and are very similar to the endings of the definite article.

Usage

Here are all endings in the *nominative*:

Deutscher Wein ist nicht teuer.
German wine is not expensive.

Deutsche Musik verkauft sich international nicht so gut.
German music doesn't sell so well internationally.

Deutsches Bier ist weltberühmt.
German beer is world famous.

Deutsche Touristen fahren gern nach Spanien.
German tourists like going to Spain.

Adjectives with the indefinite article

Here is an overview of adjective endings when the adjective is preceded by an indefinite article:

	Masculine	Feminine	Neuter	Plural
Nom.	ein gut*er* Tipp	eine gut*e* Idee	ein gut*es* Beispiel	gut*e* Pläne
Acc.	einen gut*en* Tipp	eine gut*e* Idee	ein gut*es* Beispiel	gut*e* Pläne
Dat.	einem gut*en* Tipp	einer gut*en* Idee	einem gut*en* Beispiel	gut*en* Pläne*n*
Gen.	eines gut*en* Tipps	einer gut*en* Idee	eines gut*en* Beispiels	gut*er* Pläne

Other determiners – the possessives and kein

All possessives (**mein**, **Ihr**, **unser** etc.) and the negative **kein** follow the same declension pattern as **ein**, but note that all *plural forms* end in **-en**:

Plural

Nom. – **meine/keine gut*en* Pläne**
Acc. – **meine/keine gut*en* Pläne**
Dat. – **mein*en*/kein*en* gut*en* Pläne*n***
Gen. – **mein*er*/kein*er* gut*en* Pläne**

Usage

Here are all endings in the *accusative*:

Er hat einen gut*en* Tipp für uns.
He's got a good tip for us.

Der Direktor hatte eine gut*e* Idee.
The director had a good idea.

Kannst du mir ein gut*es* Beispiel geben?
Can you give me a good example?

Sie entwarfen immer gut*e* Pläne.
They always drew up good plans.

Er hat uns keine gut*en* Pläne gegeben.
He hasn't given us any good plans.

Adjectives with the definite article

Here is an overview of adjective endings when the adjective is preceded by a definite article:

	Masculine	*Feminine*	*Neuter*	*Plural*
Nom.	der neue Film	die neue CD	das neue Auto	die neuen Schuhe
Acc.	den neuen Film	die neue CD	das neue Auto	die neuen Schuhe
Dat.	dem neuen Film	der neuen CD	dem neuen Autos	den neuen Schuhen
Gen.	des neuen Films	der neuen CD	des neuen Autos	der neuen Schuhe

Note that adjectives after the definite article only take two endings: **-e** and **-en**.

Usage

Here are all endings in the *dative*:

Bist du schon in dem neuen Film von Spielberg gewesen?
Have you been to see the new film by Spielberg yet?

Mit der neuen CD von Sting kann ich nicht viel anfangen.
The new CD by Sting doesn't mean anything to me.

Bist du mit dem neuen Auto gefahren?
Did you drive the new car?

Ich werde mit den neuen Schuhen ins Theater gehen.
I will wear my new shoes to the theatre.

Other determiners – alle, dieser *etc.*

After **alle** 'all', **dieser** 'this', **einige** 'some'/'any', **jeder** 'every', **viele** 'many' the endings of adjectives are the same as the adjectival endings with the definite article:

Jeder neue Film wird zuerst im Abaton Kino gezeigt. (*nom., masc.*)
Every new film is first shown in the Abaton cinema.

Alle neue*n* Schuhe sind mir zuerst zu eng. (*nom., pl.*)
All new shoes are at first too tight for me.

Points to watch out for

Spelling variations

When positioned before a noun, adjectives with **-au** or **-eu** (**sauer**, **teuer**) drop the **-e** before **-r**, while adjectives ending in **-el** (**dunkel**) drop the **-e** before the **-l**. Also note that **hoch** loses the letter **-c**:

Er fährt einen teuren Sportwagen.
He drives an expensive sports car.

Es war eine dunkle Nacht.
It was a dark night.

Sie sprang über den hohen Zaun.
She jumped over the high fence.

Different endings

Colours ending in **-a**, such as **lila** 'purple', **rosa** 'pink', don't take endings in standard German:

Er trägt ein rosa Hemd.
He wears a pink shirt.

Sie mag ihre lila Bluse.
She likes her purple blouse.

Adjectives constructed from names of towns end in **-er** and don't change their forms:

Der Frankfurter Hauptbahnhof wurde gerade renoviert.
The Frankfurt railway station has just been renovated.

Comparative and superlative forms of adjectives

Formation

Adjectives are frequently used in the comparative and superlative form. The comparative form is constructed by adding **-er** while the superlative is formed with **am** + **-sten**.

	Comparative		*Superlative*
billig	→ billiger	→	am billigsten
klein	kleiner		am kleinsten

Note that most monosyllabic adjectives with the stem vowel **a**, **o** or **u** also take an umlaut in both forms:

	Comparative		*Superlative*
warm	→ wärmer	→	am wärmsten
jung	jünger		am jüngsten

Usage before and after noun

When appearing *after* a noun the comparative and superlative form don't take any additional endings:

Ist die Tasche billiger?
Is that bag cheaper?

Mein Computer war am billigsten.
My computer was the cheapest.

When both forms appear directly *in front* of a noun they take the same endings as all adjectives. Note that in the superlative '**am**' is omitted:

Ich habe einen jüngeren Bruder. (*indef. art., acc., masc.*)
I have got a younger brother

Er nahm das kleinste Stück. (*def. art., acc., nom., neuter.*)
He took the smallest piece.

Spelling variations and irregular forms

Note the following spelling variations:

- In the *comparative* form adjectives ending in **-el** drop the **-e**, while adjectives ending in **-er**, drop the **-e** after **-au** and **-eu**: **dunkel – dunkler – am dunkelsten, teuer – teurer – am teuersten**.
- Adjectives ending in **-d**, **-t**, **-sch**, **-haft**, **-s**, **-ß**, **-x** and **-z** usually insert an extra **-e** in the *superlative*: **gesund – gesünder – am gesündesten, interessant – interessanter – am interessantesten**.
- **hoch**, **groß** and **nah** change their forms as follows: **hoch – höher – am höchsten, groß – größer – am größten, nah – näher – am nächsten**.
- **gut** and **viel** have quite irregular forms: **gut – besser – am besten, viel – mehr – am meisten**.

Adverbs in German

Using adverbs

While adjectives describe nouns, *adverbs* provide more information about verbs:

Adjective	**Sie ist schön.**	She is beautiful.
Adverb	**Sie singt schön.**	She sings beautifully.

Contrary to English where adverbs often differ from adjectives ('beautiful' → 'beautifully'), adverbs in German use the form of the adjectives. However, adverbs in German do not take any endings.

Comparative and superlative of adverbs

Adverbs form their *comparative* in the same way as adjectives by adding **-er**. The *superlative* forms are usually constructed with **am** + **-sten**:

Sie singt schön. → Sie singt schöner. → Sie singt am schönsten.

Note that **gern** has irregular comparative and superlative forms: **lieber, am liebsten**.

**Ich trinke gern Wasser. → Ich trinke lieber Bier. →
Ich trinke am liebsten Wein.**

Different ways of comparing – als and so . . . wie

There are two main ways of comparing in German:

- **als** is frequently used to express inequality, corresponding to the English 'than':

    Die CD ist *teurer* als *das Buch*.
    The CD is more expensive than the book.

- **so . . . wie** expresses the idea of equality and corresponds to the English 'as . . . as':

    Er ist *so* groß *wie* sein Bruder.
    He is as tall as his brother.

Exercise 15.1

The following sentences contain examples of adjectival endings with *indefinite articles* and *possessives*. Identify the case, gender and number as shown in the example below.

> Example: **Ich kaufe mir ein teures Auto.** →
> Case: *accusative*; gender: *neuter*; number: *singular*.

1   Ich begrüße einen alt**en** Freund aus Hannover. *acc, masc, sing*
2   Das ist aber eine gut**e** Idee! *nom, fem, sing*
3   Was kann ich meiner neu**en** Kollegin schenken? *dat, fem, plu*
4   Er glaubt seinem neu**en** Chef nicht. *acc, masc, sing*
5   Ein heiß**er** Tee hilft bei Erkältungen. *acc, masc, sing*
6   Sie wohnen in einem groß**en** Haus. *dat, neut, sing*
7   Das Wiener Schnitzel ist ein typisch**es** Gericht aus Österreich. *nom, neut, sing*
8   Er hilft seinen alt**en** Freunden gerne. *dat, fem, plu*
9   Sie sind gut**e** Schauspielerinnen. *nom, fem, plu*
10 Wir sprechen mit unseren alt**en** Kunden. *acc, fem, plu*

Exercise 15.2

Use the adjectives from the previous Exercise 15.1 and write out their forms with the definite article, using the same case and number as before.

> Example: **ein teures Auto** → *das* **teure Auto**

Exercise 15.3

Fill in the missing forms of the adjectives below. The first one has been done for you.

	Comparative	*Superlative*
hoch	**höher**	**am höchsten**
teuer	**teurer**	*am teuersten*
dunkel	*dunkler*	**am dunkelsten**
viel	**mehr**	*am meisten*
süß	**süßer**	*am süßesten*
interessant	*interessanter*	*am interessantesten*
nah	*näher*	*am nächsten*
best	*besser*	**am besten**

Exercise 15.4

Translate the sentences below into German.

1 The city is big and modern.
2 He loves Italian music.
3 German beer is world famous.
4 You have to read the new book about Mozart. (*Use the **Sie** form.*)
5 She is wearing her black shoes.
6 We drink only expensive wine.
7 How often do you speak with your old friends? (*Use the **du** form.*)
8 She likes the pink bag.
9 Munich is more expensive than Hamburg.
10 She is as beautiful as her sister.
11 We now have a bigger flat.
12 The film isn't better than the book.

Checklist	✓
1 When does an adjective take an ending?	
2 Can you name all adjective endings when they appear with no article?	
3 What are the two endings of adjectives when they appear with a definite article?	
4 What is the difference between the forms of adverbs in English and German?	
5 When do you use **als** and when **so . . . wie** in comparisons?	

1 Der Stadt ist groß und modern
2 Er liebt Italianische Musik
3 Deutsches Bier ist Weltberühmt
4 Sie müssen den neuen Buch über Mozart lesen
5 Sie trägt ihre schwarze Schuhen
6 Wir trinken nur teuer Wien
7 Wie oft sprichst du mit deinen alten Freunden
8 Sie mag die rosa Tasche
9 München ist teurer als Hamburg
10 Sie ist so schön als ihre Schwester
11 Jetzt haben wir eine größere Wohnung
12 Der Film ist nicht besser als den Buch

UNIT SIXTEEN
Prepositions

What are prepositions?

Prepositions are words that define the relationship between different elements in a sentence. They usually appear before a noun and its article or other determiners and give information about:

- directions: He is going *to* Frankfurt.
- positions: The key is *on* the table.
- time: The play starts *at* 8 pm.
- manner: She came *by* car.
- reasons: They went for a walk *despite* the weather.

Prepositions require different cases

English and German prepositions are very similar in the way they function. In German however, a word or words which follow a preposition have to take the appropriate case endings.

Here is an overview of the most commonly used prepositions and the case they require:

Accusative	Dative	Accusative or dative	Genitive
bis until, by	**aus** out of, from	**an** at, near, on	**statt** instead
durch through, by	**außer** apart from, out of	**auf** on (top of)	of
für for		**hinter** behind	**trotz** despite
gegen against, around, about	**bei** by (near), at	**in** in, to	**während** during
	gegenüber opposite	**neben** next to	**wegen** because of

Accusative	Dative	Accusative or dative	Genitive
ohne without	**mit** with, by (train etc.)	**über** above, over	
um at, round	**nach** after, to	**unter** under	
	seit since, for	**vor** before, in front of	
	von from, of	**zwischen** between	
	zu to		

The following sections will explain these prepositions in more detail.

Prepositions + accusative

Meaning and most common usage

Here is a summary of the most common usage of *prepositions + accusative*. Note that, depending on the context, prepositions can have more than one meaning.

- **bis** – 'until', 'by':

   Das Geschäft ist bis vier geöffnet.
   The shop is open until four.

   Es muss bis nächsten Samstag fertig sein.
   It has to be finished by next Saturday.

   Note that **bis** is often used with another preposition like **zu**, which then determines the case endings: **Bis zum Wochenende!** 'Until the weekend!'

- **durch** – 'through', 'by (means of)':

   Gehen wir durch den Park?
   Shall we go through the park?

   Er verriet sich durch seinen Akzent.
   He betrayed himself by his accent.

- **für** – 'for':

   Für ihren Sohn würde sie alles tun.
   She would do anything for her son.

Ich fahre für eine Woche nach Bayern.
I am going to Bavaria for a week.

* **gegen** – 'against', 'around', 'about':

  Ich bin nicht gegen diesen Vorschlag.
  I am not against this suggestion.

  Wir treffen uns gegen zwei Uhr.
  We'll meet around two o'clock.

  Es waren gegen 200 Leute da.
  There were about 200 people present.

* **ohne** – 'without':

  Ohne einen Stadtplan hätten wir das Hotel nie gefunden.
  Without a map we would never have found the hotel.

* **um** – 'at' (clock, times), 'round':

  Wir kommen um Viertel nach vier an.
  We arrive at quarter past four.

  Gehen wir einmal um den Block!
  Let's go once around the block.

Shortened forms

In the spoken language **durch**, **für** and **um** are often joined together with the definite article **das: durch das** → **durchs; für das** → **fürs; um das** → **ums**.

Prepositions + dative

Meaning and most common usage

Here is an overview of how *prepositions* + *dative* are most commonly used:

* **aus** – 'from', 'out of':

  Sie kommt aus Nordfrankreich.
  She comes from northern France.

  Sie sieht aus dem Fenster.
  She looks out of the window.

- **außer** – 'apart from', 'out of' (order, control etc.):

    Außer einem Sandwich hatte er nichts gegessen.
    Apart from a sandwich, he had not eaten a thing.

    Der Fahrstuhl ist außer Betrieb.
    The lift is out of order.

- **bei** – **'**by' (near to), 'for' (a specific company), 'at' (a house or person):

    Potsdam liegt bei Berlin.
    Potsdam is near Berlin.

    Er arbeitet bei BMW.
    He works for BMW.

    Ich war beim Zahnarzt.
    I was at the dentist.

- **gegenüber** – 'opposite':

    Gegenüber der Kirche liegt ein Park.
    Opposite the church is a park.

- **mit** – 'with', 'by' (means of transport), 'at' (age):

    Er geht mit seiner Frau ins Kino.
    He goes with his wife to the cinema.

    Sie fährt mit dem Fahrrad nach Hause.
    She goes home by bicycle.

    Er hat mit 18 geheiratet.
    He got married at 18.

- **nach** – **'**after', 'to' (towns and most countries):

    Nach dem Frühstück las er die Zeitung.
    After breakfast, he read the paper.

    Wir fuhren nach Italien.
    We went to Italy.

- **seit** – 'since', 'for' (referring to a period of time):

    Sie wohnt seit 1999 in New York.
    She has lived in New York since 1999.

    Ich arbeite seit zehn Jahren bei dieser Firma.
    I have been working at this firm for ten years.

Note that in German, **seit** is usually used in connection with the **present tense**.

- **von** – 'from', 'of', 'by' (often in constructions with the passive):

  Die E-Mail ist von meiner Chefin.
  The e-mail is from my employer.

  Sie ist eine alte Freundin von mir.
  She is an old friend of mine.

  Die Pläne wurden von einem Architekten entworfen.
  The plans were designed by an architect.

- **zu** – 'to' (to places or persons):

  Wie komme ich zum Supermarkt?
  How do I get to the supermarket?

  Ich gehe jetzt zu Susanna.
  I am going to Susanna's.

Note that **zu** also appears in a variety of expressions, such as **zum Frühstück** 'for breakfast', **zu Fuß** 'on foot', **zu Hause** 'at home'.

Shortened forms

Note that **bei**, **von** and **zu** are usually joined together with **dem**: **bei dem** → **beim**, **von dem** → **vom, zu dem** → **zum** and **zu der** is usually abbreviated → **zur**:

Wirst du mich vom Flughafen abholen?
Will you collect me from the airport?

Kommen Sie doch zur Party!
Do come to the party!

Prepositions + accusative or dative

There is a group of prepositions which can either take the accusative or dative case. These prepositions are called *Wechselpräpositionen* in German ('variable prepositions').

Guidelines for usage

In general the following guidelines apply when deciding which case the *Wechselpräpositionen* or 'variable prepositions' require:

- With the *accusative*
  The accusative case is used when a 'variable preposition' is connected to a verb indicating *movement* to or into a location, or expresses a *change of position*:

  Abends gingen wir *in die Kneipe*.
  In the evening we went to the pub.

  Ich stelle die Tasche *neben den Stuhl*.
  I put the bag next to the chair.

- With the *dative*
  A 'variable preposition' is followed by the dative when the verb focuses on *position* or limited *movement within* a location:

  Wir blieben den ganzen Abend *in der Kneipe*.
  We stayed the whole evening in the pub.

  Er tanzte die ganze Nacht *in der Kneipe*.
  He danced the whole night in the pub.

Meaning and most common usage

	Accusative	Dative
an – 'at', 'near', 'on'	**Ich hänge das Bild an *die* Wand.** I hang the picture on the wall.	**Das Bild hängt an *der* Wand.** The picture hangs on the wall.
auf – 'on (top of)'	**Sie legt das Geld auf *den* Tisch.** She puts the money on the table.	**Das Geld liegt auf *dem* Tisch.** The money lies on the table.
hinter – 'behind'	**Er geht hinter *den* Tisch.** He goes behind the table.	**Er steht hinter *dem* Tisch.** He stands behind the table.
in – '(in)to' (*acc.*), 'in' (*dat.*)	**Gehst du oft in *die* Bibliothek?** Do you often go to the library?	**Ich treffe dich in *der* Bibliothek.** I meet you in the library.
neben – 'next to'	**Stell dich neben *die* Tür!** Stand next to the door!	**Er steht neben *der* Tür.** He stands next to the door.
über – 'above', 'over'	**Sie hängt die Lampe über *das* Bett.** She hangs the lamp above the bed.	**Die Lampe hängt über *dem* Bett.** The lamp hangs above the bed.

	Accusative	*Dative*
unter – 'under'	**Er stellt die Schuhe unter das Sofa.** He puts the shoes under the sofa.	**Die Schuhe stehen unter dem Sofa.** The shoes are under the sofa.
vor – 'before', 'in front of'	**Sie trat vor das Publikum.** She stepped in front of the audience.	**Sie stand vor dem Publikum.** She stood in front of the audience.
zwischen 'between'	**Stell den Tisch zwischen das Sofa und den Sessel!** Place the table between the sofa and the armchair!	**Der Tisch steht zwischen dem Sofa und dem Sessel.** The table stands between the sofa and the armchair.

Shortened forms

The following *Wechselpräpositionen* are often abbreviated in less formal language:

- **an, auf, hinter, über, unter, vor** + *das* in the *accusative* →
  ans, aufs, hinters, übers, unters, vors
- **an, bei, hinter, in, über, unter, vor** + *dem* in the *dative* →
  am, beim, hinterm, im, überm, unterm, vorm

Note that only **am** and **im** are used in formal contexts.

Prepositions + genitive

Here are a few sentences with the prepositions **statt** 'instead of', **trotz** 'despite of', **während** 'during' and **wegen** 'because of' which take the genitive case:

Er antwortete statt seines Bruders.
He answered instead of his brother.

Trotz des schlechten Wetters sind sie spazieren gegangen.
They went for a walk despite the bad weather.

Er arbeitete während der Ferien.
He worked during the holidays.

Wegen des Staus kamen wir nicht weiter.
We did not get any further because of the traffic jam.

Note that in contemporary German the above prepositions are also frequently used with the dative:

Er antwortete statt seinem Bruder.
Trotz dem schlechten Wetter sind sie spazieren gegangen.
Er arbeitete während den Ferien.
Wegen dem Stau kamen wir nicht weiter.

- For an overview on cases and case endings, see Unit 4.

Exercise 16.1

Complete the sentences below by choosing an appropriate preposition from the box. The first one has been done for you.

vor gegen seit nach ~~auf~~ trotz um für
wegen zu bei in mit an

1 Sie legt die CD *auf* den Tisch.
2 Das nächste Café ist gleich __um__ die Ecke.
3 Wie findest du das Leben __in__ der Stadt?
4 Ich lebe und arbeite schon __seit__ einem Jahr hier.
5 Kommt Mario __zu__ deiner Party?
6 Petras Mann arbeitet __bei__ der Lufthansa.
7 Ich habe nichts __gegen__ seinen Plan.
8 __Für__ mich ist das kein Problem.
9 Siehst du das Bild __an__ der Wand?
10 __Mit__ sechs Jahren konnte Birgit schon lesen.
11 Sein Auto steht meistens direkt __vor__ dem Haus.
12 Ich gehe erst __nach__ den Nachrichten schlafen.
13 __wegen__ des schlechten Wetters blieben sie zu Hause.
14 __trotz__ des kalten Klimas gibt es hier Obstbäume.

Exercise 16.2

Now sort the prepositions from Exercise 16.1 according to the cases they require:

Prepositions + acc.	Prepositions + dat.	Prepositions + acc. or dat.	Prepositions + gen.
gegen um für	seit mit nach zu bei	auf vor in an	trotz wegen

Exercise 16.3

Fill in the correct endings and explain why the prepositions in the following sentences take either the *accusative* (*acc.*) or *dative* (*dat.*) case.

> Examples: **Sie legt die Tasche auf ___ Tisch.** →
> **Sie legt die Tasche auf *den* Tisch.**
> (*acc.* – the focus is on movement)
>
> **Die Tasche steht auf ___ Tisch.** →
> **Die Tasche steht auf *dem* Tisch.**
> (*dat.* – the focus is on position)

1 Gehst du oft in*s* Kino? *ins*
2 Treffen wir uns i*m* Kino? *ins*
3 Das Poster hängt an d*er* Wand. *den*
4 Hängst du das Poster an d*ie* Wand? *der*
5 Der Mann steht auf d*er* Brücke. *die dem*
6 Gehen Sie auf d*ie* Brücke. *dem*
7 Stellen Sie bitte das Fahrrad vor *die* die Tür!
8 Das Fahrrad steht vor *der* Tür.

Exercise 16.4

Translate the following sentences into German.

1 How do I get to the railway station?
2 He goes to Frankfurt by train.
3 She comes from England.

acc – motion
dat – position

4 How often do you go to the opera? (*Use the **Sie** form.*)
5 Do you walk through the park? (*Use the **du** form.*)
6 He stayed the whole day in the garden.
7 The pub is round the corner.
8 I was at the doctor's.
9 We've lived in Berlin since September.
10 She has been learning Spanish for two years.
11 I don't like working during the holidays.
12 He went for a walk despite the bad weather.

Checklist	✓
1 Can you remember which prepositions require the accusative and which require the dative?	
2 What do you need to be aware of when using the preposition **seit**?	
3 What is special about the so-called **Wechselpräpositionen**?	
4 Can you name three prepositions that take the genitive?	

UNIT SEVENTEEN
Forming questions

Two types of questions

There are two main types of questions in German:

- *yes/no-questions* which start with a verb and can be answered either in the affirmative or in the negative:

  Sprechen Sie Deutsch?
  Do you speak German?

  Ist das Ihre Tasche?
  Is that your bag?

- *w-questions* which start with a question word such as **wer** 'who', **wo** 'where', **warum** 'why' and tend to be more 'open':

  Wo wohnst du?
  Where do you live?

  Warum hast du schlechte Laune?
  Why are you in a bad mood?

Here are the two types in more detail.

Yes/no-questions

The verb is the first element

When forming a question of this type, the verb is placed in the initial position, followed by the subject:

  ***Bist* du aus Irland?**
  Are you from Ireland?

Arbeitet **sie noch bei Siemens?**
Does she still work at Siemens?

With two verbs

When there are two verbs in a yes/no-question, the *finite verb* – the verb which takes the personal ending – remains in the first position while the second verb moves to the end:

Kann **ich noch ein Bier** *haben*?
Can I have another beer?

Hat **er mit dem Rauchen** *aufgehört*?
Has he stopped smoking?

Sind **sie mit dem Flugzeug** *gekommen*?
Did they come by plane?

Difference between German and English

In English, you often need a form of the verb 'to do' when forming yes/no-questions: 'Does she still work for Siemens?'. In German, this type of structure does not exist. Yes/no-questions always start with the finite verb: ***Arbeit*et sie noch bei Siemens?**

The w-questions

Meaning and usage

Question words – often referred to as *interrogatives* – usually start with the letter **w** in German. Frequently used question words include:

wer?	who?
welcher?	which? what?
was? was für?	what? what kind of ?
wann?	when?
wo? wohin? woher?	where? where (to)? where from?
wie? wie viel? wie viele?	how? how much? how many?
wie lang? wie lange?	how long? for how long?
warum? wieso?	why?
wozu?	what for?

Here are some examples of **w**-questions:

Wann fängt der Film an?	When does the film start?
Warum essen Sie kein Brot?	Why don't you eat bread?
Wie viel kostet das?	How much does it cost?
Wer hat gerade angerufen?	Who just phoned?
Wie hast du das gemeint?	How did you mean that?

Points to watch out for

- **wie** 'how' can also correspond to the English 'what' when referring to names, telephone numbers and addresses:

Wie ist Ihr Name?	**Wie ist deine Adresse?**
What is your name?	What is your address?

  Wie ist Ihre Handynummer?
  What is your mobile telephone number?

- **wo** 'where' indicates position or location, whereas **woher** 'where from' and **wohin** 'where (to)' express movement:

  Wo ist das Brandenburger Tor?
  Where is the Brandenburg Gate?

  Woher kommt Lisa eigentlich?
  Where does Lisa actually come from?

  Wohin hast du das Buch gelegt?
  Where did you put the book?

- **was für** 'what kind of' can be followed by the nominative, accusative or dative case:

  Was für ein Mann ist er? (*nom.*)
  What kind of man is he?

  Was für einen Wagen hat er? (*acc.*)
  What kind of car does he have?

  Mit was für einem Stift schreibst du? (*dat.*)
  What kind of pen are you writing with?

The question words wer and welcher

Question words normally do not change in German. Two important exceptions are **wer** 'who' and **welcher** 'which', 'what' as their endings can vary.

wer *requires case endings*

The question words **wer** 'who' is used when referring to people. It has different forms relating to the four cases and their grammatical functions:

Nom.	**wer**	who
Acc.	**wen**	who(m)
Dat.	**wem**	who(m)
Gen.	**wessen**	whose

Here are some examples:

Wer hat das gemalt?
Who painted that?

Wen triffst du später?
Who(m) are you meeting later on?

Mit wem gehst du in die Oper?
Who are you going to the opera with?

Wessen Auto ist das?
Whose car is that?

Note that in contemporary German, the genitive form **wessen** is often replaced by a structure using the dative: **Wessen Auto ist das? → Wem gehört das Auto?**

welcher *and its case endings*

The question word **welcher** 'which', 'what' usually appears directly in front of a noun and must agree with the gender, case and number of that noun.

Here are all forms in the nominative, accusative and dative. Note that **welcher** does not exist in the genitive case.

	Masculine	*Feminine*	*Neuter*	*Plural*
Nom.	**welcher**	**welche**	**welches**	**welche**
Acc.	**welchen**	**welche**	**welches**	**welche**
Dat.	**welchem**	**welcher**	**welchem**	**welchen**

Examples:

Welcher Schauspieler gefällt dir? (*nom., masc.*)
Which actor do you like?

Welchen Saft möchten Sie? (*acc., masc.*)
Which/what juice would you like?

Bei welchem Friseur warst du? (*dat., masc.*)
Which hairdresser did you go to?

Indirect questions

Indirect questions can be a more polite way of asking for information and are often preceded by phrases such as **Können Sie mir sagen** . . . 'Can you tell me . . .' or **Wissen Sie** . . . 'Do you know . . .':

Direct question		*Indirect question*
Wie heißen Sie?	→	**Können Sie mir sagen, wie Sie heißen?**
Wann fängt der Film an?	→	**Wissen Sie, wann der Film anfängt?**

Indirect questions with ob

When transforming yes/no-questions into indirect questions, **ob** 'whether' is used:

Direct question		*Indirect question*
Kommt Mary aus Irland?	→	**Können Sie mir sagen, ob Mary aus Irland kommt?**
Kann man das Wasser trinken?	→	**Wissen Sie, ob man das Wasser trinken kann?**

Finite verb in final position

As all indirect questions are subordinate clauses, the finite verb in the indirect question moves to the end of the clause.

- For more information on questions with prepositions, see Unit 9.

Exercise 17.1

Find the appropriate yes/no-question for each of the sentences below, as shown in the example.

> Example: **Ja, er kommt aus Berlin.** → *Kommt* **er aus Berlin?**

1 Ja, das ist der billigste VW. *Ist es der billigste VW*
2 Ja, Carola hat einen neuen Freund. *Hat sie neuen Freund (einen)*
3 Ja, der Film fängt um halb acht an. *Fängt der der Film um halb acht an*
4 Ja, man kann auch mit dem Bus fahren. *Kann man auch mit dem Bus fahren*
5 Ja, davor hatte Susanne im Ausland gelebt. *hatte Susan davor im Ausland gel*
6 Ja, er wird seinen Führerschein im Mai machen. *wird er seinen Führerschein im Mai machen?*

Exercise 17.2

Here is an interview with Roland Bauer. Complete the questions with the appropriate **w**-question words (**wie, wo, wie lange** etc.).

> Example : _____ **heißt du? – Ich heiße Roland Bauer.**
> → *Wie* **heißt du? – Ich heiße Roland Bauer.**

1 *Wo* kommst du? – Ich komme eigentlich aus Bremen.
2 *Wie* alt bist du? – Ich bin jetzt 34 Jahre alt.
3 *Wie* arbeitest du denn? – Ich arbeite bei einer Bank.
4 Um *welche* Uhr beginnt dein Arbeitstag? – Normalerweise um acht Uhr.
5 Und *wann* machst du Feierabend? – So um halb sechs.
6 *Wie* fährst du dieses Jahr in Urlaub? – Ich fahre in die Toskana.
7 *Wie lange* wirst du dort bleiben? – Nur eine Woche.
8 *warum* bleibst du nicht länger? – Leider habe ich nicht länger Zeit.

Exercise 17.3

Fill in the gaps below with **wer**, **wen** or **wem** as appropriate.

1 W*er* hat heute angerufen?
2 W*en* triffst du heute Abend?
3 Gegen w*en* spielt Bayern München am Samstag?
4 W*em* sollen wir helfen?
5 W*er* kann die Frage beantworten?
6 Wissen Sie, für w*en* das Geschenk ist?

7 Er möchte wissen, mit w_en_ sie ausgeht.
8 Bei w_em_ habt ihr in Stuttgart gewohnt?

Exercise 17.4

Translate the following sentences into German.

1 Do you speak Russian? (*Use the **Sie** form.*)
2 Have you seen my new computer? (*Use the **du** form.*)
3 How much coffee do you drink per day? (*Use the **ihr** form.*)
4 What kind of dog is that?
5 How many people are coming to the party?
6 Where are you going tonight? (*Use the **ihr** form.*)
7 Who is the present for?
8 Who did you give the key to? (*Use the **du** form.*)
9 Who does the car belong to?
10 Which/what wine would you like? (*Use the **Sie** form.*)
11 Can you tell me where he is from? (*Use the **Sie** form.*)
12 Do you know how much it costs? (*Use the **du** form.*)

Checklist	✓
1 What is the position of the finite verb in yes/no-questions?	
2 Can you describe the basic structure of **w**-questions?	
3 In what way are **wer** and **welcher** different from other question words?	
4 What happens to the finite verb in indirect questions?	

UNIT EIGHTEEN
Conjunctions and clauses

Conjunctions link clauses

Conjunctions such as **und** 'and', **aber** 'but', **weil** 'because' and **während** 'while', usually link clauses together. Here are a few examples:

Clause 1	Conjunction	Clause 2
Das ist Peter	**und**	**er ist 30 Jahre alt.**
Maria kommt aus Bonn,	**aber**	**sie lebt jetzt in Frankfurt.**
Ich bleibe zu Hause,	**weil**	**ich müde bin.**
Er kocht etwas,	**während**	**sie schläft.**

Two groups of conjunctions in German

Conjunctions in German can be divided into two main groups:

- *Coordinating conjunctions* such as **und** 'and', **aber** 'but' and **oder** 'or' usually connect two main clauses. A main clause is a clause that can stand on its own:

  Das ist Peter. Er ist 30 Jahre alt.
  → **Das ist Peter** *und* **er ist 30 Jahre alt.**

  A coordinating conjunction does not affect the word order in the clause that follows – the finite verb remains the second element.

- *Subordinating conjunctions* such as **weil** 'because', **während** 'while', **dass** 'that' normally link subordinate clauses and main clauses. A subordinate clause cannot stand on its own as it is dependent on a main clause.

Subordinate conjunctions do affect the word order and normally send the finite verb to the end of the clause:

Ich bleibe zu Hause, *weil* ich müde *bin*.

Here are the different kinds of conjunctions in more detail.

Coordinating conjunctions

The most important coordinating conjunctions are:

aber	but
denn	because
oder	or
sondern	but (following a negative statement)
und	and

Meaning and most common usage

- **aber** is equivalent to the English 'but' and contrasts information from the first clause with the second clause:

  Wir wollten in München leben, aber das war uns zu teuer.
  We wanted to live in Munich but it was too expensive for us.

- **denn** introduces the second clause, which gives a reason for the action or event of the first clause and usually corresponds to the English 'because':

  Dieses Buch kann man nicht mehr kaufen, denn es ist vergriffen.
  You cannot buy this book any more because it is out of print.

- **oder** expresses an alternative or contrast, like the conjunction 'or' in English:

  Gehen wir ins Kino oder bleiben wir zu Hause?
  Are we going to the cinema or are we staying at home?

- **sondern** expresses the notion of 'but ... (instead)' and is used after a negative statement in the first clause:

  Stuttgart liegt nicht in Bayern, sondern in Baden-Württemberg.
  Stuttgart is not in Bavaria, but in Baden-Württemberg.

- **und** is the most frequently used conjunction in German und normally links words or two main clauses:

Er ernährte sich nur von Wasser und Brot.
He lived only on bread and water.

Sie studiert Medizin und ihre Schwester geht noch in die Schule.
She studies medicine and her sister is still at school.

Omitting the subject

When the same subject is used in clauses connected by **und**, **aber** and **sondern** it is often left out in the second clause:

Ich komme aus Frankfurt und (ich) bin ledig.

Wir wohnen nicht mehr in Bonn, sondern (wir) leben jetzt in Bremen.

Connecting subordinate clauses

Although **und**, **aber**, **oder** and **sondern** usually link main clauses, they can also be used to connect two subordinate clauses:

Ich hoffe, dass man nicht lange warten muss *und* dass es nicht zu viel kostet.
I hope that you don't have to wait long *and* that it doesn't cost too much.

Subordinating conjunctions

Major subordinating conjunctions

Frequently used subordinating conjunctions in German include:

als	when (*referring to an event or period in the past*)
bevor	before
bis	until
da	as, since
damit	so (that)
dass	that
nachdem	after
ob	whether (or not)
obwohl	although
sobald	as soon as
seitdem	since
während	while
weil	because

wenn	when, whenever (*present tense*)
	if (*conditional, hypothetical*)
	whenever (*referring to repeated events in the past*)

Meaning and most common usage

The following section explains the meaning and most common usages of frequently used subordinating conjunctions.

- **als** 'when' – referring to a single event or a longer period in the past:

  Wir besuchten den alten Dom, als wir in Köln waren.
  We visited the old cathedral when we were in Cologne.

  Als ich ein Kind war, spielte ich gern mit Autos.
  When I was a child I liked playing with cars.

  For repeated events, see **wenn** on page 137.

- **bevor** 'before', **bis** 'until, **nachdem** 'after', **seitdem** 'since' and **während** 'while'/'during' – referring to the sequence of events or actions:

  Du musst warten, bis du 18 bist.
  You have to wait until you are 18.

  Wasch dir die Hände, bevor du zum Essen kommst!
  Wash your hands before you start to eat!

  Nachdem sie ihren Führerschein gemacht hatte, fuhr sie nach Paris.
  After she had passed her driving test, she drove to Paris.

  Seitdem er ins Fitnessstudio geht, sieht er müde aus.
  Since he's been going to the gym, he's looking tired.

- **da** 'as', 'since' – indicating a cause:

  Da er kein Geld hat, kann er nicht ins Kino gehen.
  As he doesn't have any money he can't go to the cinema.

- **damit** 'in order to', 'so that' – describing a purpose:

  Sie schicken ihn in die USA, damit er sein Englisch verbessern kann.
  They are sending him to the USA so that he can improve his English.

- **dass** 'that' – expressing opinions, ideas, feelings etc.:

  Ich denke, dass Popstars heutzutage zu viel verdienen.
  I think that pop stars earn too much money nowadays.

- **ob** 'whether' – introduces an indirect question:

  Wissen Sie schon, ob Sie zum nächsten Meeting kommen können?
  Do you know yet whether you will be able to come to the
  next meeting?

For more information on indirect questions, see Unit 17.

- **obwohl** 'although' – expressing a contrast:

  Er hat sich ein Auto gekauft, obwohl er kein Geld hat.
  He bought a new car, although he doesn't have any money.

- **weil,** 'because' – indicating a reason:

  Sie ist sehr glücklich, weil sie verliebt ist.
  She is very happy because she is in love.

  The conjunctions **weil** and **denn** are usually interchangeable in meaning,
  but as **denn** is a coordinating conjunction the word order of the clause
  that follows is not affected.

- **wenn** 'when', 'whenever' – referring to actions or events in the present
  and future and describing repeated actions in the past:

  Wenn ich koche, höre ich immer Radio.
  When/whenever I cook, I listen to the radio.

  Wenn er ins Kino ging, aß er immer Popcorn.
  When/whenever he went to the cinema he always ate popcorn.

- **wenn** 'if' – expressing conditions:

  Wenn ich mehr Geld hätte, würde ich ein neues Auto kaufen.
  If I had more money, I would buy a new car.

Word order in subordinate clauses

As mentioned earlier, subordinating conjunctions introduce a subordinate
clause and send the finite verb to the end.

If a sentence starts with a subordinate clause, the finite verb moves to
the end of the clause and appears next to the finite verb of the main
clause:

Als ich ein Kind *war, spielte* ich gern mit Autos.
Seitdem er ins Fitnessstudio *geht, sieht* er müde aus.

Note the comma between the verbs.

Conjunctions consisting of more than one part

There are a few conjunctions which consist of more than one part. They can be divided into two main groups:

- *Coordinating conjunctions* such as **entweder ... oder** 'either ... or', **sowohl ... als (auch)** 'as well as':

  Ich fahre *entweder* in die Stadt *oder* ich bleibe zu Hause.
  Either I'm going into town or I'm staying at home.

  Sie studierte *sowohl* in Leipzig *als auch* in Cambridge.
  She studied in Leipzig as well as in Cambridge.

  In these structures the finite verb remains the second element.

- *Subordinating conjunctions* which introduce a subordinate clause where the finite verb is usually sent to the end. They include **als ob** 'as if', **so dass** 'so that', **je ... desto** 'the ... the':

  Es sah so aus, *als ob* es regnen würde.
  It looked as if it might rain.

  Es war schon spät, *so dass* er ein Taxi nach Hause nehmen musste.
  It was late so he had to take a taxi home.

  When using **je ... desto**, note that **je** introduces a subordinate clause while **desto** functions as a coordinating conjunction:

  ***Je* länger du in Madrid lebst, *desto* besser wirst du Spanisch sprechen.**
  The longer you stay in Madrid the better you will speak Spanish.

Use of commas

As mentioned above, a comma must be used to separate a subordinate clause from a main clause. This is compulsory in German.

Also note that commas are usually placed before the coordinating conjunctions **aber**, **denn** and **sondern**.

- For more information on main and subordinate clauses, see Unit 19.

Exercise 18.1

Link the sentences below by using **aber**, **denn**, **oder**, **sondern** or **und**.

Example: **Sie kann den Tee nicht bezahlen. Sie hat ihr Portmonee verloren.**
→ **Sie kann den Tee nicht bezahlen, *denn* sie hat ihr Portmonee verloren.**

1 Wir fahren nicht mit dem Bus. Wir gehen zu Fuß. *sondern*
2 Meine Familie lebt noch in Wien. Ich wohne jetzt in London. *aber*
3 Sie kocht zuerst die Suppe. Dann deckt sie den Tisch. *und*
4 Ich studiere nicht mehr. Ich arbeite jetzt. *sondern*
5 Die Leute wollen schlafen gehen. Sie sind sehr müde. *denn*
6 Möchtest du jetzt nach Hause? Möchtest du noch in eine Kneipe gehen? *oder*

Exercise 18.2

Use the subordinating conjunction in brackets to form a new sentence.

Example:

Wir kaufen einen neuen Fernseher. Der alte ist kaputt. (weil)
→ **Wir kaufen einen neuen Fernseher, *weil* der alte kaputt ist.**

1 Sie möchte Ärztin werden. Sie kann kein Blut sehen. (obwohl)
2 Meine Mutter gab mir immer ein Glas Milch. Ich ging ins Bett. *gehe* (bevor)
3 Ich bin mir nicht sicher. Ich kann morgen kommen. (ob)
4 Matthias ging oft ins Theater. Er lebte in Berlin. (als)
5 Er soll weniger essen. Er ist zu dick. (da)
6 Sie macht einen Computerkurs. Sie verbessert ihre Berufschancen. (damit)

Exercise 18.3

Complete the following sentences by using either **als** or **wenn**.

1 Immer _wenn_ es heiß war, bekam ich ein Eis.
2 _Als_ er sie zum ersten Mal besuchte, brachte er ihr Blumen mit.
3 Susanne heiratete, _als_ sie noch zur Schule ging.

4 _Wenn_ du morgen Zeit hast, gehen wir chinesisch essen.
5 _Als_ ich meinen Computerkurs begann, war ich überrascht, wie
   einfach es war.
6 Jedes Mal _wenn_ ich nach London fuhr, regnete es.

Exercise 18.4

Translate the sentences below into German. _(put correct conjunction)_

sondern 1 Basel isn't in Austria but in Switzerland.
aber 2 The children are tired but they don't want to go to bed.
dass 3 He thinks that footballers earn too much money.
dass 4 I hope that it doesn't rain.
als 5 When I was a child I lived in Florida.
wenn 6 Whenever I hear this music I want to dance.
wenn 7 When you are in London you must eat 'fish and chips'. (_Use the **Sie**
   form._)
oder 8 He wants to study either music or mathematics.
oder 9 We can either go by car or by train.
denn 10 The longer you live in Berlin the better you will understand German.
   (_Use the **Sie** form._)

Checklist	✓
1 What are the main differences between coordinating and subordinating conjunctions?	
2 Can you name five coordinating conjunctions?	
3 Can you explain the differences between **als** and **wenn** when referring to the past?	
4 How would you say 'either . . . or' and 'the more, the better' in German?	

UNIT NINETEEN
Word order and sentence structure

German word order – rules and patterns

This unit gives you an overview of the basic principles regarding word order in German and deals with the following:

- the position of the *verb* in various sentence structures
- the position of the *subject* and the *direct* and *indirect* objects
- the sequence of different elements in a sentence.

Position of verb in different sentence structures

The position of the verb depends on the type of sentence used. There are four basic types:

Main clauses	**Jürgen *arbeitet* bis fünf Uhr.**
Subordinate clauses	**Ich hoffe, dass wir den Zug nicht *verpassen*.**
Imperative	***Gehen* Sie jetzt!**
Questions	***Kommt* sie bald?**

In the next sections all the above structures are shown in more detail.

Verbs in main clauses

Principal feature – the finite verb is the second element

A main clause is a sentence that can stand on its own. The finite verb – the verb that takes the personal ending – is usually the second element.

Subject	Finite verb	Other elements
Katja	**beginnt**	**heute ihren Englischkurs.**
Unsere Freunde	**kommen**	**nach dem Essen zu Besuch.**

Subject–verb inversion

The finite verb also remains in second position when a sentence starts with an element other than the subject:

First element	Finite verb	Subject	Other elements
Heute	**beginnt**	**Katja**	**ihren Englischkurs.**
Nach dem Essen	**kommen**	**unsere Freunde**	**zu Besuch.**

This change of word order is called the *subject–verb inversion*. Note that the first element can consist of one word like **heute** 'today', or several words such as **nach dem Essen** 'after the meal'.

Word order with two verbs

When there are two verbs in a main clause, the second verb moves to the end while the finite verb still forms the second element. This pattern can be found in various structures, for instance in sentences with *modal verbs*, in the *present perfect tense* and in *passive* constructions:

Subject	Finite verb	Other elements	Second verb
Katja	**kann**	**heute ihren Englischkurs**	**beginnen.**
Nach dem Essen	**sind**	*unsere Freunde zu Besuch*	**gekommen.**
Das Haus	**wurde**	**vor 10 Jahren**	**gebaut.**

Constructions with three verbs

When three verbs are part of a main clause, the finite verbs stays in the second position and the other two verbs move to the end:

Subject	Finite verb	Object and other elements	Final verbs
Ich	**habe**	**leider nicht**	**helfen können.**
Du	**wirst**	**wohl mehr Sport**	**treiben müssen.**

Note that sentences with three verbs usually contain a modal verb, which takes the infinitive form and appears in the final position. For more details, see Unit 7, pages 54–6.

Verbs in subordinate clauses

Dependent on a main clause

A subordinate clause has to be linked to a main clause as it cannot stand on its own:

Er fährt nach Frankfurt, weil er einen alten Freund besuchen möchte.
He is travelling to Frankfurt because he wants to visit an old friend.

In the above example the subordinate clause (**..., weil er einen alten Freund besuchen möchte**) shows its dependent character as it would not make sense without the preceding main clause (**Er fährt nach Frankfurt, ...**).

Different types of subordinate clauses

A subordinate clause is usually introduced by a subordinate conjunction such as **dass** 'that', **weil** 'because' etc. Two other types of subordinate clauses are:

- *indirect questions* which are introduced by **ob** 'whether' or question words such as **wer** 'who', **warum** 'why' etc.
- *relative clauses* which are introduced by relative pronouns such as **der** 'who', **deren** 'whose' etc.

Finite verb – final position

In all types of subordinate clauses, the finite verb moves to the end of the clause. Note that the main and the subordinate clause are *always* separated by a *comma*:

Main clause	Subordinate clause	Finite verb
Ich denke,	**dass er aus Berlin**	**kommt.**
Das ist der Mann,	**der einen Volvo**	**fährt.**
Ich weiß nicht,	**warum sie schlechte Laune**	**hat.**

More than one verb in a subordinate clause

In subordinate clauses with two verbs, the second verb appears before the finite verb:

Sie hofft, dass sie das Abschlussexamen *bestehen wird*.
She hopes that she will pass the final exam.

When using three verbs in a subordinate clause, the finite verb normally is at the end of the clause:

Ich weiß nicht, ob die E-Mail schon *abgeschickt worden ist.*
I don't know whether the e-mail has been sent yet.

Verbs in zu + infinitive clauses

The infinitive in final position

In **zu** + *infinitive* clauses, the verb in the infinitive form appears at the end.

Er hofft, im Lotto zu *gewinnen.*
He hopes to win the lottery.

Ich habe keine Zeit, ins Kino zu *gehen.*
I don't have time to go to the cinema.

Ist es schwierig, Karten zu *kaufen?*
Is it difficult to buy tickets?

zu + *infinitive* clauses often follow verbs such as **aufhören** 'to stop', **hoffen** 'to hope', **versuchen** 'to try' and expressions which consist of verb + noun (**Ich habe keine Zeit ...**) or verb + adjective (**Ist es schwierig ...**).

The construction um zu – *'in order to'*

When using the construction **um zu** 'in order to', **um** is at the beginning of the clause, while **zu** + infinitive appears at the end: **Er läuft viel, um fit zu bleiben**. 'He runs a lot (in order) to stay fit.'

Verbs in the imperative

Finite verb in the first position

In the imperative or command form the finite verb is usually the first element. This pattern applies to all *three* imperative forms in German:

Setz **dich!**	Sit down!	(*du* form)
Esst **nicht so viel!**	Don't eat so much!	(*ihr* form)
Notieren **Sie das!**	Write this down!	(*Sie* form)

When used in connection with another verb, the second verb normally moves to the end:

Geh jetzt einkaufen!
Go shopping now!

Verbs in questions

There are two main types of question in German – yes/no-questions and w-questions. The finite verb is placed in different positions:

- *yes/no-questions* start with the finite verb:

    ***Spielen* Sie ein Instrument?**
    Do you play an instrument?

- *w-questions* usually start with a question word. The finite verb is the second element:

    Was *machst* du heute Abend?
    What are you doing tonight?

- For more information on questions, see Unit 17.
- For more information on relative clauses, see Unit 20.

Position of subject in main and subordinate clauses

The subject in main clauses

A German sentence or main clause often starts with the subject, followed by the finite verb:

Subject	Finite verb	Object or other elements
Ich	**gehe**	**heute Abend ins Kino.**
Peter	**fährt**	**meistens mit dem Auto zur Arbeit.**

Subject–verb inversion

However, another element such as an expression of time or place can come at the beginning of a sentence. In this case the subject moves from its first position and goes directly after the finite verb.

First element	Finite verb	Subject	Object and other elements
Heute Abend	**gehe**	**ich**	**ins Kino.**
Zur Arbeit	**fährt**	**Peter**	**immer mit dem Auto.**

The subject in subordinate clauses

Note that in subordinate clauses the subject usually comes directly after the conjunction:

Ich hoffe, dass *ich* im Sommer nach Frankreich fahren kann.
I hope that I can travel to France this summer.

Sie trank noch ein Bier, weil *sie* großen Durst hatte.
She drank another beer because she was very thirsty.

Position of direct and indirect objects

The sequence in which direct and indirect objects appear in a sentence depends on their being either a noun or a pronoun:

- If there are two nouns, the *indirect object* (in the dative case) comes *before* the *direct object* (accusative):

    Er kauft seiner *Frau* (*indirect object*) einen *Ferrari*. (*direct object*)
    He buys his wife a Ferrari.

- When a noun appears together with a pronoun, the pronoun always precedes the noun, regardless of the case:

    Er kauft ihn (*dir. obj.*) seiner Frau. (*ind. obj.*)
    He buys it for his wife.

    Er kauft ihr (*ind. obj.*) einen Ferrari. (*dir. obj.*)
    He buys her a Ferrari.

- If both objects appear as pronouns, the direct object comes first:

    Er kauft ihn (*dir. obj.*) ihr. (*ind. obj.*)
    He buys it for her.

Starting the sentence with an object

In order to shift the emphasis in a sentence, the direct or indirect object can become the first element:

Wir schicken *die Rechnung* nächste Woche.
→ ***Die Rechnung* schicken wir nächste Woche.**

Expressions of time, manner, place

The time–manner–place rule

Expressions describing *when*, *how* or *where* something happens usually appear in the following sequence: time–manner–place.

Subject	Finite verb	Time	Manner	Place	Final verb
Susi	**fährt**	**später**	**mit dem Auto**	**nach Hause.**	
Tom	**hat**	**heute**	**allein**	**im Labor**	**gearbeitet.**

Acting as the first element

It is possible for any one of these expressions to form the first element in a sentence. The other elements usually remain in the same positions:

Heute hat Tom allein im Labor gearbeitet.

Im Labor hat Tom heute allein gearbeitet.

Allein hat Tom heute im Labor gearbeitet.

Note that in German there is *no comma* between the first element and the rest of the sentence.

Exercise 19.1

Link the two sentences by using the conjunction in brackets. Don't forget to change the word order accordingly.

Example: **Er will Deutsch lernen. Er hat jemanden aus Leipzig kennen gelernt. (weil)**
→ **Er will Deutsch lernen, *weil* er jemanden aus Leipzig kennen gelernt hat.**

1 Wir sind jeden Abend ins Café gegangen. Wir haben in Rom gewohnt. (als)
2 Julia spielt oft mit den Kindern. Sie hat sehr viel zu tun. (obwohl)
3 Paul darf fernsehen. Er hat seine Hausaufgaben gemacht. (nachdem)
4 Wir konnten im Restaurant nicht rauchen. Es war verboten. (weil)
5 Ich glaube ihm nicht. Er hat fünf Kilo abgenommen. (dass)
6 Er hat in Berlin gearbeitet. Er ist nach London gezogen. (bevor)

Exercise 19.2

Now rewrite the sentences in Exercise 19.1 by starting with the conjunction:

Example:

Er will Deutsch lernen, *weil* er jemanden aus Leipzig kennen gelernt hat.
→ *Weil* er jemanden aus Leipzig kennen gelernt *hat*, *will* er Deutsch lernen.

Exercise 19.3

The sentences are all mixed up. Put the words in the correct order. Start with the word or words in italics:

Example:

Kathrin – *nächstes Wochenende* – besuchen – ihren Freund – wird
→ Nächstes Wochenende wird Kathrin ihren Freund besuchen.

1 *ich* – morgen – mit meiner Mutter – fahre – nach Hannover
2 gehen – wir – noch schnell – *heute Nachmittag* – auf den Markt – müssen
3 geben – ihr – *den Ring* – er – nächste Woche – will
4 werden – *im Sommer* – sie – in den Bergen – alle zusammen – wandern gehen
5 *du* – ausgegangen – im letzten Jahr – bist – ziemlich oft
6 musste – *stundenlang* – sie – am Bahnhof – auf ihren Zug – warten
7 schenkten – *wir* – eine Flasche französischen Rotwein – ihnen
8 wollte – ihr – sagen – nicht – *er* – es

Exercise 19.4

Translate the sentences below into German. Note that sometimes there might be more than one possible answer.

1 Go now! (*Use the **du** form.*)
2 He is going to the cinema tonight.
3 I will give you my keys. (*Use the **du** form.*)
4 Next week, Margret will start her computer course.
5 After the meal, Matthias went for a walk.
6 Unfortunately, I could not send you the report. (*Use the **Sie** form.*)
7 She worked the whole morning in the kitchen on her own.
8 I hope that we can go to Austria this winter.
9 I don't know why he went to Hamburg.
10 He doesn't know whether he will pass the final exam.

Checklist	✓
1 Can you name the four types of basic sentences?	
2 What is the position of the finite verb in main and subordinate clauses?	
3 What does subject–verb inversion mean?	
4 Can you explain the sequence of expressions that describe *when*, *how* or *where* something happens?	

UNIT TWENTY
Relative clauses

What are relative clauses?

Relative clauses are subordinate clauses which provide more information about a noun or phrase in the main clause. They are usually introduced by *relative pronouns*, words such as 'who', 'whose' in English and **die**, **dessen** in German:

Das ist die alte Frau, *die* in unserer Straße wohnt.
This is the old woman who lives in our street.

Da geht der Mann, *dessen* Auto gestohlen wurde.
There goes the man whose car was stolen.

Relative pronouns – an overview

List of all relative pronouns

Here are all the relative pronouns:

	Masculine	Feminine	Neuter	Plural
Nom.	der	die	das	die
Acc.	den	die	das	die
Dat.	dem	der	dem	denen
Gen.	dessen	deren	dessen	deren

Note that the forms of relative pronouns are similar to the definite articles. Only the dative plural (**denen**) and all the genitive forms differ in their endings.

Using the correct relative pronoun

In German, the relative pronoun has to agree in gender (*masculine, feminine or neuter*) and number (*singular, plural*) with the preceding noun it refers to.

Note that the case of the relative pronoun depends on its function *within the clause* it introduces. If, for instance, the relative pronoun functions as the *subject* in the relative clause it has to take the appropriate *nominative* form:

Sie sahen einen Film, *der* in den 50er Jahren gedreht wurde.
They watched a film, which was made in the 1950s.

The function of the relative pronoun within the relative clause becomes clear, when you convert it into a statement:

→ **Der Film** (*subject, nominative*) **wurde in den 50er Jahren gedreht.**

Equally, if the relative pronoun refers to the *direct object*, it needs to take the appropriate *accusative* form:

Ist das der Mantel, *den* du gestern gekauft hast?
Is this the coat which you bought yesterday?
→ **Du hast *den Mantel*** (*direct object, accusative*) **gestern gekauft.**

In the following sections, you will find more details on relative clauses in all four cases.

Relative clauses in more detail

Using the nominative

When the relative pronoun is the subject of the relative clause its form is identical with the *definite article* in the nominative case:

Er trug einen Anzug, *der* sehr teuer war. (*masc.*)
He wore a suit which was very expensive.

Sie hat eine Freundin, *die* aus London kommt. (*fem.*)
She has a friend who comes from London.

Das Boot ist ein Buch, *das* von Buchheim geschrieben wurde. (*nt.*)
Das Boot is a book which was written by Buchheim.

Ich kann Leute nicht ausstehen, *die* andere ungerecht behandeln. (*pl.*)
I can't stand people who treat others unjustly.

Using the accusative

In the case of the relative pronoun functioning as the direct object or following a preposition (requiring the accusative) the usual accusative endings of the definite articles apply. They are identical with the nominative forms, except for *masculine* nouns (**den**):

Erkennst du den Schauspieler, *den* wir gerade gesehen haben? (*masc.*)
Do you recognise the actor we saw just now?

Ist das die Frau, *die* du von früher kennst? (*fem.*)
Is this the woman you used to know?

Wie findest du das Hemd, *das* ich gestern gekauft habe? (*nt.*)
What do you think of the shirt I bought yesterday?

Wir besuchen unsere Freunde, die wir lange nicht gesehen haben. (*pl.*)
We are visiting our friends who(m) we haven't seen for a long time.

Using the dative

When the relative pronoun functions as an indirect object within a clause it requires the dative forms. This also applies when the relative pronoun relates to a preposition or verb requiring the dative case.

Kennst du Peter, *dem* ich 100 Euro geliehen habe? (*masc.*)
Do you know Peter who(m) I lent 100 euro(s)?

Wir haben eine alte Nachbarin, *der* wir gern helfen. (*fem.*)
We have an elderly neighbour we like to help.

Dort drüben ist das Haus, in *dem* ich früher gewohnt habe. (*nt.*)
Over there is the house I used to live in.

Da sind Sylvia and Kurt, mit *denen* wir in den Urlaub gefahren sind. (*pl.*)
There are Sylvia and Kurt who we went on holiday with.

Using the genitive

Relative pronouns in the genitive, corresponding to the (English) 'whose', indicate a relationship of belonging between persons or things:

Das ist Jörg, *dessen* **Sohn Musik studiert.** (*masc.*)
This is Jörg whose son studies music.

Da drüben ist Petra, *deren* **Mann allein in den Urlaub gefahren ist.** (*fem.*)
Over there is Petra whose husband went on holiday on his own.

Das ist das Kind, *dessen* **Eltern beide aus den USA kommen.** (*nt.*)
This is the child whose parents come from the USA.

Ein Stipendium bekommen nur die Studenten, *deren* **Eltern nicht so viel verdienen.** (*pl.*)
Only those students whose parents aren't so well off get a grant.

Points to watch out for

Usage in German and English

The relative pronoun is often omitted in English, as can be seen from some of the examples above, e.g.:

Do you recognise the actor we saw just now?

In German, the relative pronoun *cannot* be omitted, e.g.:

Erkennst du den Schauspieler, *den* **wir gerade gesehen haben?**

No distinction between 'who' and 'which'

Also note that there is no distinction in German between 'who' and 'which'. The same relative pronouns refer to persons *and* things:

Das ist Karl, *der* **aus Berlin kommt.**

Sie sahen einen Film, *der* **in den 50er Jahren gedreht wurde.**

Finite verb in final position

As relative clauses are subordinate clauses the finite verb goes to the end:

Das ist die alte Frau, die in unserer Straße *wohnt*.

Da sind Sylvia and Kurt, mit denen wir in den Urlaub gefahren *sind*.

Relative clauses are *always* preceded by a *comma*.

The relative pronoun was

Referring to a whole phrase

In order to refer to a phrase rather than just a noun the relative pronoun **was** 'which' introduces the relative clause:

Sie arbeitet jetzt nur vormittags, was **ich gut finde.**
She now works only in the morning which I think is good.

Sie möchten nach Australien fliegen, was **sehr teuer ist.**
They want to fly to Australia which is very expensive.

In connection with alles, etwas, nichts

was is also used when referring to the pronouns **alles** 'everything', **etwas** 'something', **nichts** 'nothing' in the main clause.

Sie konnte sich an *nichts* erinnern, *was* vor dem Unfall passiert war.
She couldn't remember anything that had happened before the accident.

Alles, was **sie sagte, machte Sinn.**
Everything she said made sense.

Das ist *etwas*, *was* ich nicht ausstehen kann.
That is something I cannot stand.

- For more information on subordinate sentence structure, see Unit 19.

Exercise 20.1

Complete the following relative clauses with the appropriate relative pronoun in the nominative.

Example: **Das ist Matthias, _____ Busfahrer ist.**
→ **Das ist Matthias, *der* Busfahrer ist.**

1 Das ist mein Mann, _der_ bei der Dresdner Bank arbeitet.
2 Sie hat eine Tochter, _die_ Maria heißt.
3 Der Rhein ist ein Fluss, _der_ durch Köln fließt. _der_
4 Kennst du das Kaufhaus, _das_ sich neben dem Bahnhof befindet?
5 Das sind Monika und Karl, _die_ im Lotto gewonnen haben.
6 Die Universität hat viele Studenten, _die_ aus China kommen.

Exercise 20.2

Complete the following relative clauses with the relative pronouns in the box below. The first one has been done for you.

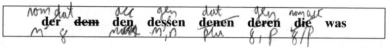

der	dem	den	dessen	denen	deren	die	was

1 Das ist mein Kugelschreiber, mit *dem* du schreibst.
2 Mimi heiratet einen Mann, _den_ sie im Urlaub kennen gelernt hat.
3 Wer sind die Leute, auf _die_ er wartet?
4 Siehst du meine Kollegin, von _der_ ich dir erzählt habe?
5 Er kennt den Gitarristen, _dessen_ Sohn auch Musiker ist.
6 Das ist Caroline, _deren_ Tochter gerade in die Schule gekommen ist.
7 Das sind die Mitarbeiter, mit _denen_ wir am nächsten Projekt arbeiten.
8 Alles, _was_ Sie mir zuschicken wollten, ist nicht angekommen.

Exercise 20.3

Form relative clauses containing the following information about Joachim Manner from Vienna. Start each sentence with '**Das ist Joachim Manner, …**'.

Example: **Joachim Manner lebt in Wien.**
→ **Das ist Joachim Manner, *der in Wien lebt.***

1 Er war früher ein Wiener Sängerknabe.
2 Seine Eltern kommen aus Tirol.

3 Joachim spielt auch sehr gut Klavier.
4 Für ihn komponierte ein Kollege ein Lied.
5 Von ihm gibt es zahlreiche CDs.
6 Seine Freundin ist auch Sängerin.

Exercise 20.4

Translate the following sentences into German.

1 I am reading a book which was written by Heinrich Böll.
2 Is this the table you bought last week? (*Use the **Sie** form.*)
3 There is my uncle who(m) I lent my car.
4 That is the woman who(m) I work with.
5 This is Dietrich whose son is a pop singer.
6 Do you know Claudia whose children study in Munich? (*Use the **du** form.*)
7 She would like to work abroad which I find good.
8 Everything he said made sense.

Checklist	✓
1 Can you name the relative pronoun in all four cases?	
2 What determines the case of the relative pronoun?	
3 What happens to the finite verb in a relative clause?	
4 Which relative pronoun would you use when referring to a whole phrase?	

UNIT TWENTY-ONE
Negative constructions

Two main forms for negatives – nicht **and** kein

There are two main ways of constructing negatives in German – using
nicht or **kein**:

Das verstehen wir nicht.
We don't understand that.

Er hat kein Auto.
He doesn't have a car.

Here are both forms in more detail.

nicht **in more detail**

When to use nicht

Nicht is used in negative constructions with adjectives and verbs:

Der Wein war *nicht teuer*. (*adjective*)
The wine was not expensive.

Es *funktioniert nicht*. (*verb*)
It doesn't work.

It is also used with nouns connected to a definite article or possessive:

Das ist *nicht der Sohn* von Paul. (*def. art.*)
That is not Paul's son.

Das ist *nicht meine Tasche*. (*possessive*)
This is not my bag.

nicht *can negate more than one word*

nicht can negate a whole sentence or only a part of it:

> **Ich komme morgen *nicht*.**
> I won't be coming tomorrow.

> **Er fährt *nicht* mit seiner Frau nach Paris.**
> He is not going to Paris with his wife.

In the first sentence **nicht** refers to the whole sentence ('I won't come'), in the second only to one part ('his wife'). It is understood that he will go to Paris, but not with his wife.

Position of nicht

The position of **nicht** in a sentence depends on whether the whole sentence or only parts of it are negated and what other elements, such as adjectives or expressions of time, the sentence contains.

Negating a whole sentence
When negating a whole sentence, **nicht** can appear in several positions.

- **nicht** normally moves to the end in simple structures with a *direct* or *indirect object* or an *expression of time*:

Sie kaufte den Fernseher.	**Sie kaufte den Fernseher *nicht*.**
Sie helfen den Leuten.	**Sie helfen den Leuten *nicht*.**
Er kommt heute.	**Er kommt heute *nicht*.**

- It precedes expressions of *manner* (how?) and *places*:

Er fuhr mit dem Auto.	→ **Er fuhr *nicht* mit dem Auto.**
Susi studiert in Paris.	→ **Susi studiert *nicht* in Paris.**

- **nicht** is normally placed directly before an *adjective*:

Peter war gestern krank.	→ **Peter war gestern *nicht* krank.**

- In structures which consist of more than one verb, **nicht** usually appears in front of the second verb:

Sie hat die CD gekauft.	→ **Sie hat die CD *nicht* gekauft.**
Er kann morgen kommen.	→ **Er kann morgen *nicht* kommen.**

- When used with *separable verbs*, **nicht** has to come directly before the separated prefix:

  Maria holt Bernd ab. → **Maria holt Bernd *nicht* ab.**

Negating parts of a sentence

When **nicht** refers to a specific part in a sentence, it is usually placed directly before the relevant element:

Claudia hat *nicht* am Sonntag ihre Schwester besucht.

The sentence implies that she visited her sister, but not on Sunday.

Other negatives – nie, niemals

Other frequently used negative words in German are **nie** 'never' and its slightly more formal alternative **niemals**:

Gaby geht nie ins Kino.
Gaby never goes to the cinema.

Er war niemals in Berlin.
He's never been to Berlin.

The pronoun nichts

Nichts is the pronoun form of **nicht** and corresponds to the English '(not) anything' or 'nothing':

Das bedeutet nichts.   **Ich höre nichts.**
This doesn't mean anything.   I don't hear anything.

kein in more detail

When to use kein

The negative **kein** is used with nouns appearing with an indefinite article or with no article:

Das ist eine gute Idee.   →   **Das ist keine gute Idee.**
Haben Sie Zeit?   **Haben Sie keine Zeit?**

Different endings of kein

kein follows the declension pattern of the indefinite article. It must agree in gender, number and case with the noun. Here are all the endings of **kein**:

	Masculine	Feminine	Neuter	Plural
Nom.	kein Computer	keine Zeit	kein Geld	keine Kinder
Acc.	keinen Computer	keine Zeit	kein Geld	keine Kinder
Dat.	keinem Computer	keiner Zeit	keinem Geld	keinen Kindern
Gen.	keines Computers	keiner Zeit	keines Geldes	keiner Kinder

Examples:

Paula hat keinen Computer.	(*accusative, masculine*)
Clara hat keine Zeit.	(*accusative, feminine*)
Wir haben kein Geld.	(*accusative, neuter*)
Sie haben keine Hobbys.	(*accusative, plural*)

kein used as a pronoun

kein can be used as a pronoun when it stands in for a noun. Here are all forms:

	Masculine	Feminine	Neuter	Plural
Nom.	keiner	keine	keins	keine
Acc.	keinen	keine	keins	keine
Dat.	keinem	keiner	keinem	keinen
Gen.	keines	keiner	keines	keiner

Examples:

Ist das eine Digitalkamera?	→	**Nein, das ist keine.** (*nom., fem.*)
Hat er Geld?		**Nein, er hat keins.** (*acc., neuter.*)
Haben Sie Kinder?		**Nein, wir haben keine.** (*acc., pl.*)

nicht **or** kein

In a few circumstances either **nicht** or **kein** can be used. This is the case when referring to professions, languages and activities relating to sport:

Sie ist Architektin. – Sie ist nicht/keine Architektin.
Er spricht Italienisch. – Er spricht nicht/kein Italienisch.
Herr Krause spielt Tennis. – Herr Krause spielt nicht/kein Tennis.

Exercise 21.1

Answer the following sentences in the negative, using the negation with **nicht** or **kein**.

Examples: **Haben Sie einen DVD-Spieler?**
→ **Nein, ich habe** *keinen* **DVD-Spieler.**

War sie gestern in der Kneipe?
→ **Nein, sie war gestern** *nicht* **in der Kneipe.**

1 Ist er morgen im Büro?
2 Finden sie das eine gute Idee?
3 Hast du Lust ins Theater zu gehen?
4 Werdet ihr Montag arbeiten?
5 Macht er eine Reise nach Italien?
6 Haben Sie gefrühstückt?
7 Seid ihr gestern Abend ins Konzert gegangen?
8 Spricht er eigentlich Chinesisch?

Exercise 21.2

Complete the sentences below by adding the correct form of the pronoun **kein**.

Example: **Wir brauchen Geld für unseren Urlaub, aber wir haben _____ .**
→ **Wir brauchen Geld für unseren Urlaub, aber wir haben** *keins.*

1 Er ist ein guter Rugbyspieler, ich bin _____ .
2 Angela ist eine gute Zuhörerin, aber Isabella ist _____ .

3 Wir suchen einen neuen Fernseher, denn wir haben _____ .
4 Alle meine Freunde trinken Bier, nur ich trinke _____ .
5 Alle haben Zeit, nur ich habe _____ .
6 Haben sie Kinder? Nein, sie haben _____ .

Exercise 21.3

Complete the following German expressions by supplying the appropriate forms of **kein**. The gender and number are given in brackets.

>   Example: **Wir hatten _____ Chance.** (*fem., sing.*)
>   → **Wir hatten *keine* Chance.**

1 Das wird dir _____ Glück bringen. (*nt., sing.*)
2 Es macht _____ Sinn. (*masc., sing.*)
3 Ich habe _____ Ahnung. (*fem., sing.*)
4 Das geht auf _____ Fall. (*masc., sing.*)
5 Das Kind hat _____ Manieren. (*pl.*)
6 _____ Mensch fragt danach. (*masc., sing.*)

Exercise 21.4

Translate the following sentences into German.

1 She is not going to Vienna.
2 We haven't bought the house.
3 She won't be coming tomorrow.
4 They never go to the pub.
5 You don't say anything. (*Use the du form.*)
6 He has nothing to say.
7 They don't have children.
8 She has no time for hobbies.
9 Last year he had a dog but now he hasn't got one.
10 I have a mobile phone for him but he doesn't want one.

Checklist	✓
1 When do you normally use **nicht** and when **kein**?	
2 What is the general position of **nicht** when negating a part of a sentence?	
3 Do you know two other negatives apart from **nicht** and **kein**?	
4 When can you use either **nicht** or **kein**?	

UNIT TWENTY-TWO
The passive voice

Differences between active and passive

The passive, also called the passive voice, stands in contrast to the active (voice):

- A sentence in the _active_ stresses who or what is the 'doer' of the action:

  Der Gärtner gießt die Blumen.
  The gardener is watering the flowers.

- The focus of a sentence in the _passive_ is on the action, not the 'doer':

  Die Blumen werden vom Gärtner _gegossen_.
  The flowers are being watered by the gardener.

Formation – an overview

Most passive constructions in German consist of the appropriate form of **werden** + _past participle_ of the relevant verb:

Der Bundestag _wird_ alle vier Jahre _gewählt_.
The German Parliament is elected every four years.

Der Oscar _wurde_ von Martin Scorsese _gewonnen_.
The Oscar was won by Martin Scorcese.

The formation, usage and the different tenses of the passive will be explained in the following sections.

The passive in the present tense

Formation

In the present tense the passive is constructed with the present tense of **werden** + *past participle* of the relevant verb. Note that **werden** is an irregular verb. Here are all the forms:

Ich *werde* gefilmt.	Wir *werden* gefilmt.
Du *wirst* gefilmt.	Ihr *werdet* gefilmt.
Sie *werden* gefilmt.	Sie *werden* gefilmt.
Er *wird* gefilmt.	Sie *werden* gefilmt.

Usage

The passive in the present tense form is often used when referring to events that happen regularly and when giving instructions, for instance in manuals or cookery books:

Fasching wird im Februar gefeiert.
Carnival is celebrated in February.

Dann werden die Schrauben angezogen.
Then the screws are tightened.

Das Mehl wird zuletzt beigemengt.
The flour is added last.

Note that **werden** as the finite verb is usually the second element, while the past participle moves into the final position.

of 'werden'

The passive in the past tenses

The simple past is preferred *(präteritum)*

Although the passive voice exists in all three past tenses, it is usually used in the *simple past tense*. It is constructed with the simple past tense of **werden** + *past participle*:

Ich *wurde* gefilmt.	Wir *wurden* gefilmt.
Du *wurdest* gefilmt.	Ihr *wurdet* gefilmt.
Sie *wurden* gefilmt.	Sie *wurden* gefilmt.
Er/Sie/Es *wurde* gefilmt.	Sie *wurden* gefilmt.

Simple past – usage

The passive in the simple past is used in a wide range of contexts, from everyday situations to historical events:

Das Fußballspiel wurde verschoben.
The football match was postponed.

Das Penicillin wurde von Alexander Fleming entdeckt.
Penicillin was discovered by Alexander Fleming.

1990 wurden Ost- und Westdeutschland wieder vereinigt.
In 1990, East and West Germany were reunited.

Present perfect *(Präsens)*

The passive in the present perfect is constructed with the appropriate present tense form of **sein** + *past participle* of the relevant verb + **worden**:

Ich bin noch nicht untersucht worden.
I haven't been examined yet.

Das Stadion ist zweimal umgebaut worden.
The stadium has been/was rebuilt twice.

Note that this present perfect structure is often replaced with the simple past tense:

Das Stadion ist zweimal umgebaut worden.
→ **Das Stadion wurde zweimal umgebaut.**

Past perfect *(Plusquamperfekt)*

The passive in the past perfect tense is constructed with the *simple past tense* of **sein** + *past participle* of the relevant verb + **worden**. It is normally used in more formal contexts, such as reports or articles:

(Präteritum von 'sein')

Er war bereits vor fünf Jahren festgenommen worden.
He had already been arrested five years ago.

The passive in the future tense

When forming the passive in the future tense, **werden** appears twice as both the future tense *and* the passive use **werden** in their formation.

Since the repetition of **werden** is considered to be stylistically inelegant, the *present tense form of the passive +* an *indication of time* is often used instead:

Future passive:	**Das Gebäude wird renoviert werden.** →
Present tense:	**Das Gebäude wird _bald_ renoviert.**
	The building will soon be renovated.

Future passive:	**Die Pläne werden besprochen werden.** →
Present tense:	**Die Pläne werden _in der nächsten Sitzung_ besprochen.**
	The plans will be discussed during the next meeting.

Points to watch out for

Prepositions in passive constructions – von, durch and mit

In order to indicate by whom or what an action is done, the preposition **von** has to be used:

Er wurde von einem Polizisten verhaftet.
He was arrested by a policeman.

Two other prepositions often used in passive structures are **durch**, which expresses by what means the action is carried out and **mit**, which identifies what implement is being used:

Das Haus wurde durch einen Brand zerstört.
The house was destroyed by fire.

Er wurde mit einem Messer getötet.
He was killed with a knife.

Note that the preposition **durch** requires the accusative; **von** and **mit** are followed by the dative case.

Using the correct case

When transforming a sentence into a passive construction, the *direct object* (accusative) of the active sentence usually becomes the subject in the passive version:

Der Vater holt *den Sohn* (*direct object*) **ab.**   →
The father collects the son.

Der Sohn (*subject*) **wird vom Vater abgeholt.**
The son is collected by the father.

As the subject of the passive sentence has to be in the nominative case, the appropriate nominative form has to be used.

Verbs taking the dative

A verb taking the dative needs a different structure in the passive. The dative object moves to the beginning of the passive sentence and is followed by the relevant form of **werden**. Here are a few examples:

Der Frau **wird von den Kindern geholfen.**
The woman is being helped by the children.

Mir **wurde geraten, mehr Sport zu treiben.**
I was advised to do more sport.

Ihm **wurde eine Taschenuhr geschenkt.**
He was given a watch.

Ihnen **wurde zu ihrem Lottogewin gratuliert.**
They were congratulated on their lottery win.

Omitting the 'doer'

Note that passive constructions do not always reveal who or what initiated the action. This omission occurs in order to focus more on the action itself rather than on the 'doer':

Das Meeting wurde abgesagt.
The meeting was cancelled.

Werden Sie schon bedient?
Are you being served?

Using man as an alternative to the passive

It is possible to replace a passive construction by using **man** as part of an active sentence:

Es wird gesagt, Irland ist sehr schön.	→ **Man sagt, Irland ist sehr schön.**
It is said that Ireland is very beautiful.	People say Ireland is very beautiful.

Das Problem wurde geregelt.	→ **Man regelte das Problem.**
The problem resolved.	Somebody resolved the problem.

Note that the alternative structure with **man** is commonly used in German.

The passive with sein

In a few instances, the passive in German is formed with the appropriate form of **sein** + *past participle*. In contrast to the German passive with **werden** which describes an action or a process, the **sein**-passive focuses on the state of a person or thing, often as a result of an action carried out previously:

Action	*Result*
Der Tisch *wird* gedeckt.	→ **Der Tisch *ist* gedeckt.**
The table is being laid. (i.e. at this moment).	The table is laid (i.e. as a result of it having been laid).
Das Geschäft *wird* geschlossen.	→ **Das Geschäft *ist* geschlossen**.
The shop is being closed.	The shop is closed.
Die Stadt *wurde* wieder aufgebaut.	→ **Die Stadt *war* wieder aufgebaut.**
The city was being rebuilt.	The city was rebuilt again.

Note that this form of the passive is much less used than the passive with **werden** and usually occurs in the present and simple past tense.

Exercise 22.1

Supply the appropriate form of **werden** in the *present tense*.

> Example: **Ich _____ vom Bürgermeister begrüßt.**
> → **Ich *werde* vom Bürgermeister begrüßt.**

1 Du wirst hier sehr gut behandelt.
2 Ich werde von einem Gewitter aufgeweckt.

3 Die Mona Lisa _wird_ von allen bewundert. *wurde*
4 Wir _werden_ von Annie Leibovitz für ein Magazin fotografiert. *wurden*
5 Das Frühstück _wird_ ab sieben Uhr serviert. *wurde*
6 Die Patienten _werden_ mit Naturprodukten behandelt. *wurden*
7 _werdet_ ihr von euren Eltern abgeholt? *wurdet*
8 Die Maschinen _werden_ in China produziert. *wurden*

Exercise 22.2

Write out the above sentences from Exercise 22.1 in the *simple past tense*.

> Example: **Ich _____ vom Bürgermeister begrüßt.**
> → **Ich *wurde* vom Bürgermeister begrüßt.**

Exercise 22.3

Convert the following sentences about the company *Adidas* into the passive. Use the *simple past tense*.

> Examples: **1949 gründete Adolf Dassler die Firma Adidas.**
> → *1949 wurde die Firma Adidas von Adolf Dassler gegründet.*
>
> **Zuerst stellte man Sportschuhe her.**
> → *Zuerst wurden Sportschuhe hergestellt.*

wurde ausgestattet 1 1954 stattete Adidas die deutsche Fußballnationalmannschaft aus.
wurden produziert 2 Ab 1963 produzierte man auch Fußbälle.
wurde veröffentlicht 3 1986 veröffentlichte die Band Run DMD den Song *My Adidas*.
wurde geleitet 4 In den 80er-Jahren leitete Käthe Dassler die Firma.
wurde verbreitet 5 Anfang der 90er-Jahre verbreitete Madonna das Adidas-Logo.
wurde erweitert 6 In den 90er-Jahren erweiterte man auch das Sortiment.
wurden gekauft 7 1997 kaufte die Salomon Gruppe die Firma Adidas auf.
wurden gesponsert 8 Adidas sponserte mehrere Fußballweltmeisterschaften.

Ab 1963 Fußbälle wurden auch produziert

Exercise 22.4

Translate the sentences below into German.

1 The president is elected every five years. *wird gewählt*
2 We are being filmed. *werden gefilmt*
3 Are you being served? (*Use the du, Sie and ihr forms.*) *Werden bedient*

Wir werden gefilmt

4 Christmas is celebrated in December. *wird gefeiert*
5 The meeting was cancelled. *wurde Versammlung abgesagt*
6 The Oscar was won by Julia Roberts. *wurde gewonnen*
7 The song will be sung by Will Smith. *wird gesungen werden*
8 The church was destroyed by a fire. *wurde zerstört*

Checklist	✓
1 Can you explain the difference between the active and passive (voice)?	
2 Which verb is normally used to form the passive in German?	
3 Which two tenses are usually used when using the passive in German?	
4 When do you use the preposition **von** in passive construction?	

UNIT TWENTY-THREE
Subjunctive forms

What is the subjunctive?

The subjunctive 'mood' of a verb stands in contrast to a verb in the indicative 'mood'. While the indicative form states facts: 'I am at home', the subjunctive is often used in imagined situations, such as wishful thinking: 'If only I *were* at home'.

Two subjunctive forms in German

There are two different subjunctive forms in German, *Konjunktiv II* and the less common *Konjunktiv I*:

- *Konjunktiv I* is based on the *infinitive* form of the verb and usually occurs in indirect speech to indicate what somebody has said:

   Er sagte, er *sei* krank.
   He said he was ill.

- *Konjunktiv II* derives its form from the *simple past tense* and is often used in hypothetical situations and conditional sentences:

   Dann *hätte* ich mehr Zeit.
   Then I'd have more time.

   Wenn ich reich *wäre*, *müsste* ich nicht arbeiten gehen.
   If I were rich I wouldn't have to go to work.

It can also be used to express wishes and to add a degree of politeness:

   Ich *wünschte*, du *wärest* hier.
   I wish you were here.

Könnten Sie mir sagen, wo das Rathaus ist?
Could you tell me where the town hall is?

Furthermore, the _Konjunktiv II_ forms can also be used in reported speech.

This unit will deal with the formation and usage of _Konjunktiv II_. For more information on _Konjunktiv I_ and _Konjunktiv II_ in indirect speech, see Unit 24.

Konjunktiv II – formation

Präteritum

Regular verbs

The _Konjunktiv II_ forms of regular verbs are identical to the _simple past tense_ forms. They are constructed with the _stem_ of the _verb_ + the following endings: **ich -_te_, du -_test_, Sie -_ten_, er/sie/es -_te_, wir -_ten_, ihr -_tet_, Sie -_ten_, sie -_ten_**:

te
test
te
tet
ten
ten

An deiner Stelle _trainierte_ ich mehr.
In your position/If I were you, I'd train more.

Ich _wünschte_, du _rauchtest_ weniger.
I wish you'd smoke less.

Irregular verbs

The _Konjunktiv II_ forms of irregular verbs are formed with the _simple past stem_ + endings listed below. In addition, an _umlaut_ is placed wherever possible. Here are a few examples including the frequently used verbs **haben, sein** and **werden**:

		gehen	_kommen_	_haben_	_sein_	_werden_
		ging-	**kam-**	**hatt-**	**war-**	**wurd-**
ich	-e	ging**e**	käm**e**	hätte	wäre	würde
du	-(e)st	ging**est**	kämest	hättest	wär(e)st	würdest
er/sie/es	-e	ging**e**	käm**e**	hätte	wäre	würde
wir	-en	ging**en**	käm**en**	hätten	wären	würden
ihr	-(e)t	ging**t**	käm**et**	hättet	wär(e)t	würdet
sie/Sie	-en	ging**en**	käm**en**	hätten	wären	würden

e
est
e
en
t
en

Ich *ginge* gern öfters ins Kino.
I'd like to go to the cinema more often.

An deiner Stelle *würde* ich früher aufstehen.
In your position/If I were you I'd get up earlier.

Modal verbs

The *Konjunktiv II* forms of modals are constructed with the *stem* of the *infinitive* + the **-te** endings used for regular verbs. Only **mögen** changes its stem slightly:

[handwritten: → möchte]

	dürfen	*können*	*mögen*	*müssen*	*sollen*	*wollen*
ich	dürfte	könnte	möchte	müsste	sollte	wollte
du	dürftest	könntest	möchtest	müsstest	solltest	wolltest
er/sie/es	dürfte	könnte	möchte	müsste	sollte	wollte
wir	dürften	könnten	möchten	müssten	sollten	wollten
ihr	dürftet	könntet	möchtet	müsstet	solltet	wolltet
sie/Sie	dürften	könnten	möchten	müssten	sollten	wollten

[handwritten in left margin: te, test, te, ten, tet, ten]

Mixed verbs

Mixed verbs which share characteristics of regular and irregular verbs add an umlaut to their past simple stem and take the *Konjunktiv II* endings of regular verbs. They include:

bringen	→	brachte	brächte	to bring
denken		dachte	dächte	to think
wissen		wusste	wüsste	to know

Konjunktiv II – usage

As pointed out before, the *Konjunktiv II* forms of verbs are used in a variety of contexts. Here are the most important ones.

Hypothetical situations

Konjunktiv II expresses ideas and situations which are not real but just imagined, often indicating a possibility:

Dann hätte ich mehr Zeit.
Then I'd have more time.

Da gäbe es mehrere Möglichkeiten.
There would be several possibilities.

Conditional sentences

Conditional sentences, when expressing imagined conditions and unreal consequences, use *Konjunktiv II*:

Wenn ich mehr Zeit hätte, ginge ich öfters spazieren.
If I had more time I'd go for a walk more often.

Wenn ich im Lotto gewänne, machte ich eine Weltreise.
If I won the lottery I'd go on a trip around the world.

Konjunktiv II also occurs in sentences which contain phrases such as **Wenn ich Sie/du wäre ...** 'If I were you ...' and **An Ihrer/deiner Stelle ...** 'In your position'/'If I were you ...' and is frequently used when giving advice:

An Ihrer Stelle machte ich mir nicht so viel Sorgen.
In your position/If I were you I wouldn't so worry much.

Wenn ich du wäre, ginge ich mal zum Friseur.
If I were you I'd go to the hairdresser.

Expressing wishes

Konjunktiv II is often used in connection with wishes. These sentences also often start with **wenn**:

Wenn sie doch bloß pünktlicher wäre!
If only she were more punctual!

Wenn er nur bald nach Hause käme!
I wish he'd come home soon!

Adding politeness

Konjunktiv II can add a tone of politeness to a question or request and also frequently appears with indirect questions:

Wären Sie bereit, länger zu arbeiten?
Would you be prepared to work longer?

Könnten Sie mir sagen, wie viel Uhr es ist?
Could you tell me what time it is?

Indirect speech

For information on the use of *Konjunktiv II* in indirect speech, see Unit 24.

Replacing *Konjunktiv II* with würden + infinitive

In contemporary German, especially in the spoken language, it is common to replace the *Konjunktiv II* form of many regular and irregular verbs with **würden** + *infinitive*:

Dann hätte ich mehr Zeit.
→ **Dann *würde* ich mehr Zeit *haben*.**

hätte = würde ____ haben

Wenn ich im Lotto gewänne, machte ich eine Weltreise.
→ **Wenn ich im Lotto gewinnen würde, *würde* ich eine Weltreise *machen*.**

Referring to the past

Konjunktiv II can also relate to events and situations in the past:

Hätte ich damals nur nichts gesagt!
If only I hadn't said anything at the time!

Sie wären gern noch länger geblieben.
They would have liked to have stayed longer.

Formation

This past tense is constructed with the *Konjunktiv II forms* of **haben** or **sein** + the *past participle* of the relevant verb:

***Hätte* er doch nur länger *geschlafen*!**
If only he had slept longer!

Wenn wir zu Fuß *gegangen wären*, wäre *nichts passiert*.
If we had gone on foot nothing would have happened.

Using a modal verb

When using a modal verb in the *Konjunktiv II* in the past with another verb, both verbs move to the end of the clause and are in the infinitive:

Du hättest wirklich ein bisschen netter *sein können*.
You really could have been a bit nicer.

Wenn er mehr trainiert hätte, hätte er schneller *laufen können*.
If he had trained more he could have run faster.

Exercise 23.1

Complete the *Konjunktiv II* forms of all verbs in the table below:

	machen	*kommen*	*können*	*haben*	*sein*	*werden*
ich	machte	käme	könnte	hätte	wäre	würde
du	machtest	kämest	könntest	hättest	wärest	würdest
er/sie/es	machte	käme	könnte	hätte	wäre	würde
wir	machten	kämen	könnten	hätten	wären	würden
ihr	machtet	kämet	könntet	hättet	wärt	würdet
Sie/sie	machten	kämen	könnten	hätten	wären	würden

Exercise 23.2

Give advice to people by using the *Konjunktiv II* form of the verb in brackets. Start the sentence with '**An deiner Stelle . . .**'.

Examples:

Ich schlafe schlecht. (früher ins Bett gehen)
→ **An deiner Stelle *ginge* ich früher ins Bett.**

Mein CD-Spieler ist kaputt. (einen neuen CD-Spieler kaufen)
→ **An deiner Stelle *kaufte* ich einen neuen CD-Spieler.**

1 Ich habe Kopfschmerzen. (ein Aspirin nehmen)   *hätte nehmen*
2 Ich würde gern das Konzert von Blumfeld sehen   *hätte besorgen*
   (Karten besorgen)

3 Ich habe einen Bierbauch. (weniger Bier trinken) *hätte getrunken*
4 Ich habe lange nichts von Jörg gehört. (ihm eine E-Mail
   schreiben) *hätte geschrieben*
5 Meine Haare sind zu lang. (zum Friseur gehen) *wäre gegangen*
6 Claudia sieht sehr gestresst aus. (mit ihr sprechen) *hätte gesprochen*
7 Mein Herz tut manchmal weh. (mit dem Rauchen aufhören) *hätte aufgehört*
8 Mein Computer ist schon wieder kaputt. (einen neuen Computer
   kaufen) *kaufte*
9 Ich habe Ärger mit meiner Freundin. (ihr Blumen mitbringen) *hätte mitgeben*
10 Ich fühle mich nicht fit. (mehr Sport treiben) *hätte getrieben*

Exercise 23.3

Now rewrite the sentences by using **würden** + *infinitive* instead of
Konjunktiv II:

   Examples:

   An deiner Stelle ginge ich früher ins Bett.
   → **An deiner Stelle *würde* ich früher ins Bett *gehen*.**

   An deiner Stelle kaufte ich einen neuen CD-Spieler.
   → **An deiner Stelle *würde* ich einen neuen CD-Spieler *kaufen*.**

Exercise 23.4

Translate the following sentences into German. Use both *Konjunktiv II*
and **würden** + *infinitive*.

1 I'd like to go to the theatre more often. *würde gehen*
2 In your position I'd train more. (*Use the Sie form.*) *würden to üben*
3 Then I'd have more time. *würde haben*
4 If only she were more punctual! *würde sein*
5 In your position I'd drink less beer. (*Use the du form.*) *würdest trinken*
6 In your position I wouldn't worry so much. (*Use the Sie form.*) *würden sorgen*
7 If I won the lottery I'd go on a trip around the world. *würde gehen*
8 I wish you were here. (*Use the du form and Konjunktiv II only.*)

würdest wünschen

Checklist	✓
1 Can you name four instances when *Konjunktiv II* is used in German?	
2 Do you know how to construct the *Konjunktiv II* forms of regular and irregular verbs?	
3 How would you say 'If I were you . . .' and 'In your position . . .'?	
4 How can you replace the *Konjunktiv II* forms?	

UNIT TWENTY-FOUR
Indirect speech

Direct and indirect speech

There are two ways of reporting what somebody said. One way is to use the exact words of the other person. In writing, this is done by putting the original words in quotation marks (*direct speech*).

The other way is to incorporate the original words into a sentence (*indirect speech*):

Direct speech	**Sie sagte: „Ich bin glücklich.“**
	She said, 'I am happy.'
Indirect speech	**Sie sagte, sie sei glücklich.**
	She said she was happy.

Indirect speech in English and German

Changing tenses in English

In English, indirect speech is mainly signalled by a shift in tense:

She said, 'I am happy.'   →   She said she *was* happy.
He said, 'I need more money.'   He said he *needed* more money.

Specific verb form in German – Konjunktiv I

German however has a specific verb form, *Konjunktiv I*, to indicate what somebody said:

Sie sagte: „Ich bin glücklich.“   →   **Sie sagte, sie *sei* glücklich.**
Er sagte: „Ich brauche mehr Geld.“   **Er sagte, er *brauche* mehr Geld.**

The formation and usage of *Konjunktiv I* will be explained in the following sections.

Konjunktiv I – formation

No stem change

The *Konjunktiv I* of both regular and irregular verbs is constructed with the *stem* of the verb in the *infinitive* + the *appropriate endings*. Irregular verbs in this construction do **not** change their stem vowel.

		leben	*fahren*	*haben*	*sein*
		leb-	*fahr-*	*hab-*	*sei-*
ich	-e	leb*e*	fahr*e*	hab*e*	sei
du	-(e)st	leb*est*	fahr*est*	hab*est*	sei(*e*)*st*
er/sie/es	-e	leb*e*	fahr*e*	hab*e*	sei
wir	-en	leb*en*	fahr*en*	hab*en*	sei*en*
ihr	-(e)t	leb*t*	fahr(e)*t*	hab*t*	sei*et*
Sie/sie	-en	leb*en*	fahr*en*	hab*en*	sei*en*

Note that **sein** doesn't add an **-e** in the **ich** and **er/sie/es** forms.

Konjunktiv I – usage

Konjunktiv I *in use*

Konjunktiv I is mainly used in written texts such as newspaper articles, reports, essays etc. to signal indirect speech.

Here are some examples of how *direct speech* can be transformed into *indirect speech*, using a *Konjunktiv I* construction:

Direct speech	**Madonna sagte: „Ich wohne gern in London."**
Indirect speech	**Madonna sagte, sie wohne gern in London.**
	Madonna said she liked living in London.
Direct speech	**Sie betonten: „Wir sind nur gute Freunde."**
Indirect speech	**Sie betonten, sie seien nur gute Freunde.**
	They emphasised they were only good friends.

Note that in German, there is always a *comma* separating the two parts of the sentence in indirect speech.

Using dass *with* Konjunktiv I

It is also possible to use the conjunction **dass** for all the above examples:

> **Madonna sagte,** *dass* **sie gern in London wohne.**
> **Sie betonten,** *dass* **sie nur gute Freunde seien.**

Konjunktiv I *in longer passages*

In newspaper articles, reports, essays etc., it is not uncommon to find the *Konjunktiv I* verb form used throughout longer passages:

> **Beate Schulz behauptete, sie leb*e* gern in einer Wohngemeinschaft. Zuerst einmal, weil es billiger *sei*, aber auch, weil sie es nicht mög*e*, wenn sie nach Hause komm*e* und eine leere Wohnung vorfind*e*. Beate find*e* es so schön, dass man immer mit jemandem zusammen reden und essen könn*e* . . .**

Beate Schulz claimed she liked living in shared accommodation. First because it was cheaper, she said, but also because she didn't like coming home to an empty flat. Beate added, she thought it was so nice to always be able to talk to someone and to eat together . . .

Note that in German, the distinctive *Konjunktiv I* form makes the context of indirect speech clear without having to add a reporting phrase like 'she added' etc. to every sentence.

Direct speech in the past

When the direct speech is in the *present perfect* or the *simple past tense*, the *Konjunktiv I* form of **haben** or **sein** + the *past participle* of the relevant verb is used:

> **Er sagt: „Ich habe ein Taxi genommen."**
> **Er sagt: „Ich nahm ein Taxi."** →
> **Er sagt, er** *habe* **ein Taxi** *genommen.*

> **Petra erklärte: „Ich bin letztes Wochenende in Paris gewesen."**
> **Petra erklärte: „Ich war letztes Wochenende in Paris."** →
> **Petra erklärte, sie** *sei* **letztes Wochenende in Paris** *gewesen.*

Replacing Konjunktiv I *with* Konjunktiv II

When the *Konjunktiv I* form is identical with the verb in the indicative, it is usually replaced with the *Konjunktiv II* form to avoid confusion with direct speech. This is the case when the plural form **sie** is used:

Direct speech	**Sie sagten: „Wir *leben* in Berlin."**
Konjunktiv I	**Sie sagten, sie *leben* in Berlin.**
	(*identical verb form*)
Konjunktiv II	**Sie sagten, sie *lebten* in Berlin.**
	(*different verb form*)

Indirect speech in less formal language

Whereas the formation of the reported speech in formal writing is to a certain degree standardised, the rules or conventions for the spoken language and less formal writing are much less strict.

Although it is always grammatically correct to use the *Konjunktiv I* form in order to report what somebody has said, its use is often perceived as stilted and old fashioned.

The following alternatives are possible in contemporary German:

- **dass** + indicative   → **Sie sagte, *dass* sie zur Party *kommt*.**
- the *indicative*   → **Sie sagte, sie *kommt* zur Party.**
- **würden** + *infinitive*   → **Sie sagte, sie *würde* zur Party *kommen*.**
- *Konjunktiv II*   → **Sie sagte, sie *käme* zur Party.**
- **dass** + *Konjunktiv II*   → **Sie sagte, *dass* sie zur Party *käme*.**

Learning tip

Although in general the use of the *Konjunktiv* forms are decreasing in contemporary German, they are still widely used in the media.

Being able to identify the various ways of indirect speech will make it much easier to understand German newspaper articles and other news reports.

> - For more information on the formation and usage of *Konjunktiv II*, see Unit 23.

Exercise 24.1

Write out the *Konjunktive I* forms for **er/sie/es** and **sie** '(they)' of the following verbs:

1 haben 2 sein 3 arbeiten 4 leben 5 geben 6 sehen 7 müssen 8 können

[handwritten:] habe sei arbeite lebe gabe soh müsste könnte
haben seien arbeiten leben gaben sohen müsstes könntes

Exercise 24.2

Convert the following sentences from indirect speech into direct speech as shown in the examples below.

> Examples:
>
> **Peter sagte, er müsse für das nächste Fußballspiel trainieren.**
> → **Peter sagte: „Ich muss für das nächste Fußballspiel trainieren."**
>
> **Meine Schwester Regine meinte, sie lebe gern in Düsseldorf.**
> → **Meine Schwester Regine meinte: „Ich lebe gern in Düsseldorf."**

1 Anke sagte, sie müsse am Wochenende arbeiten.
2 Peter meinte, er sei ein guter Schüler.
3 Meine Freundin sagte, sie könne sehr gut Ski fahren.
4 Johannes betonte, er solle keinen Alkohol mehr trinken.
5 Der Manager sagte, er habe keine Zeit für lange Meetings.
6 Herr und Frau Burger erwähnten, sie seien im August im Schwarzwald.

Exercise 24.3

The following is an excerpt from an interview with Metin Somyürek, a Turkish youngster from Berlin. Transfer what he has said into indirect speech. Use *Konjunktiv I* and complete sentences 2–7 below. The first one has been done for you.

> Example:
>
> **„Zumindest gibt es einen Jugendklub in der Nähe."**
> **1 Er sagte, ...**
> → **Er sagte, zumindest *gebe* es einen Jugendklub in der Nähe.**

„(1) Zumindest gibt es einen Jugendklub in der Nähe. (2) Der Klub hat ein gutes Angebot an Computerspielen und auch einen Fitnessraum. (3)

Dort sieht man viele andere türkische, aber selten deutsche Jugendliche. (4) Dies ist eigentlich schade. (5) Es ist nicht leicht für Türken hier in Berlin. (6) Man nennt meinen Bezirk zwar oft Klein-Istanbul, aber so richtig zu Hause fühle ich mich nirgendwo. (7) In Deutschland bin ich Türke und in der Türkei bin ich Deutscher."

2 Außerdem meinte er, der Klub . . .
3 Er erklärte, dort . . .
4 Er sagte, dies . . .
5 Außerdem erwähnte er, es . . .
6 Er sagte, man . . .
7 Er betonte, in Deutschland . . .

Exercise 24.4

Translate the sentences below into German using *Konjunktiv I*.

1 Klaus said he needed more money.
2 He said she lived in France.
3 Susanna said she was tired.
4 Angela emphasised she had to work on Saturday.
5 The manager said he had no time for hobbies.
6 They emphasised they were very happy.

Checklist	✓
1 What is the main difference between English and German when forming sentences in indirect speech?	
2 How do regular and irregular verbs form *Konjunktiv I* in German?	
3 When is it better to use *Konjunktiv II* in indirect speech instead of *Konjunktiv I*?	
4 Can you name two indirect speech constructions used in less formal German ?	

KEY TO EXERCISES
AND CHECKLISTS

UNIT 1: Nouns and gender

Exercise 1.1

Masculine	*Feminine*	*Neuter*
der Frühling	die Universität	das Exil
der König	die Fabrik	das Mädchen
der Pfennig	die Ewigkeit	das Tischlein
der Humanismus	die Freiheit	das Museum
der Schwächling	die Religion	das Video
der Motor	die Reise	das Thema
der Zyklus	die Tortur	das Element
der Honig	die Rechnung	das Büro
der Diamant	die Eleganz	das Instrument
der Konsonant	die Bedeutung	das Auto

Exercise 1.2

Masculine: -ig, -us, -or, -ant; feminine: -tät, -ik, -keit, -heit, -ion, -e, -ur, -ung, -anz, -ung; neuter: -il, -chen, -lein, -um, -o, -ma, -ment.

Exercise 1.3

1 feminine, der Rhein; 2 masculine, das Labor; 3 neuter, die Schweiz; 4 feminine, das Mädchen; 4 masculine, das Wasser.

Exercise 1.4

1 Der Mercedes ist sehr schnell. 2 Was kostet das Auto? 3 Die Zeitung kostet 1 Euro. 4 Hier ist die Mutter, aber wo ist das Mädchen? 5 Wann

beginnt das Meeting? 6 Hier ist der Tee ohne Milch. 7 Das Wasser kommt aus Frankreich. 8 Das Computerspiel war interessant. 9 Kennen Sie Herrn Schmidt? 10 Meine Damen und Herren!

Checklist

1 Certain endings of nouns and particular groups of nouns can indicate the gender of nouns. 2 Masculine: **-ant**, **-ast**, **-ich**, **-ig**, **-ling**, **-or**, **-us**. Feminine: **-a**, **-anz**, **-ei**, **-enz**, **-heit**, **-ie**, **-ik**, **-ion**, **-keit**, **-schaft**, **-tät**, **-ung**, **-ur**. Neuter: **-chen**, **-il**, **-lein**, **-ma**, **-ment**, **-o**, **-um**. 3 A compound noun can be a combination of a noun + noun(s) or can consist of adjective, preposition or verb + noun(s). The noun which forms the last element determines the gender of the compound noun. 4 Weak nouns take the ending **-n** or **-en** in all forms of the accusative, dative and genitive cases and in the plural. They usually refer to male people or animals.

UNIT 2: Plural of nouns

Exercise 2.1

2 -n, 3 (no ending), 4 -e, 5 ¨er.

Exercise 2.2

1 die Berufe 2 die Füße 3 die Spiegel 4 die Städte 5 die Kulturen 6 die Friseurinnen 7 die Gehälter 8 die Telefone 9 die Bilder 10 die Jahre 11 die Radios 12 die Hotels 13 die PCs 14 die Manager 15 die Zentren 16 die Themen 17 die Parks 18 die Firmen 19 die Regale 20 die Wälder.

Exercise 2.3

1 Ich arbeite drei Tage pro Woche. 2 Er mag Blumen. 3 Die Partys sind am Freitag und Samstag. 4 Die zwei Firmen sind in Frankfurt. 5 Die Leute kommen aus Paris. 6 Wir besuchen die Kirchen und dann die Museen. 7 Die Hotels sind modern. 8 Wir brauchen zwei Computer. 9 Die Kinder lesen zusammen. 10 Sie spielt mit den Kindern.

Checklist

1 They usually add an **-e** or **-e** + **umlaut**. 2 Most feminine nouns take the ending **-(e)n**. 3 Most foreign words add an **-s**. 4 The five main forms end in **-e**, **-(e)n**, **-er**, **-s** or have **no ending**. The plural forms that end in **-e**, **-er** and those with **no ending** can have an additional **umlaut**. 5 They add **-n** whenever possible.

UNIT 3: Articles and other determiners

Exercise 3.1

1 X, der; 2 das, X; 3 X, eine; 4 der, X; 5 dem, X; 6 der, X.

Exercise 3.2

1 deine; 2 ihrer; 3 Ihren; 4 seiner; 5 eure; 6 euren.

Exercise 3.3

1 diesen; 2 diesem; 3 solches; 4 Einige; 5 alle; 6 allen; 7 viele; 8 viel.

Exercise 3.4

1 Nach dem Mittagessen gehen wir spazieren. 2 Sie lieben das Leben.
3 Sie ist Londonerin. 4 Hast du deine Tasche gefunden?/Haben Sie Ihre
Tasche gefunden?/Habt ihr eure Tasche gefunden? 5 Ich verstehe diese
Frage nicht. 6 Ich habe diesen Film nicht gesehen. 7 Er trinkt viel Kaffee.
8 Sie hat viele Freunde. 9 Solchen Unsinn habe ich schon lange nicht
mehr gehört. 10 Alle Freunde waren da.

Checklist

1 Other important determiners are the *possessives* (**mein**, **dein** etc.), the
demonstratives (**dieser** etc.) and *indefinites* (alle, einige, jeder, viele)
2 In German, the definite article appears with some abstract nouns,
with street names, institutions, with months, seasons and infinitive verbs
used as nouns. 3 In German, when stating an affiliation to a country,
city, profession or religion no indefinite article is used. 4 Determiners
in German show the gender, number and function of a noun within a
sentence.

UNIT 4: Cases

Exercise 4.1

1 Who works at the weekend at Telekom? → *The student*: subject, nominative; 2 What did I buy in a boutique? → *This jacket*: subject, nominative;
3 Who(m) do I call in Salzburg? → *My son*: direct object, accusative;
4 Who does the father give the mobile to? → *To the daughter*: indirect
object, dative; 5 In whose shop does Hans work? → *His uncle's*: possession, gentive; 6 Who(m) do I want to visit? → *My brother*: direct object,

accusative; 7 Who have we written an e-mail to? → *Our boss*: indirect object, dative; 8 Whose DVD player does he repair? → *His parents'*: possession, genitive.

Exercise 4.2

1 eine; 2 d*er*; 3 ein*en*; 4 d*en*; 5 sein*er*; 6 d*em*; 7 d*en*; 8 ein*er*; 9 d*er*; 10 d*em*; 11 ihr*er*; 12 ein*en*; 13 ein*es*; 14 ein*es*.

Exercise 4.3

1 Das Büro *von meinem* Mann liegt im Stadtzentrum. 2 Die Managerin *von meiner* Firma kommt aus Stuttgart. 3 Man kann das Drehbuch *von diesem* Spielfilm kaufen. 4 Ich finde das Computerspiel *von meinem* Sohn zu schwer. 5 Er kannte alle Namen *von den* Teilnehmer*n*.

Exercise 4.4

1 Das ist ein Auto. 2 Das Auto ist sehr teuer. 3 Er hat einen Sohn und eine Tochter. 4 Kennst du/Kennen Sie den Sohn oder die Tochter? 5 Er gibt seiner Freundin eine CD. 6 Sie kaufte ihrem Bruder eine Flasche Wein. 7 Sie haben ein Haus mit einem Garten. 8 Es ist mir kalt./Mir ist kalt. 9 Heute ist Peters Geburtstag./Heute ist der Geburtstag von Peter. 10 Das ist der Computer meines Bruders./Das ist der Computer von meinem Bruder.

Checklist

1 The nominative, accusative, dative, genitive. 2 The nominative. 3 The accusative case is used for the direct object and the dative case for the indirect object. 4 Cases can also be triggered by certain verbs. All prepositions require either the accusative, dative or genitive. 5 The genitive is often substituted with a dative construction.

UNIT 5: Pronouns

Exercise 5.1

1 es; 2 er; 3 sie; 4 es; 5 sie; 6 er.

Exercise 5.2

1 Ja, sie kennt ihn. 2 Ja, es ist für sie. 3 Ja, ich esse ihn ganz auf. 4 Ja, sie haben ihr gedankt. 5 Ja, sie gefällt ihm. 6 Ja, sie helfen ihnen immer.

Exercise 5.3

1 meins; 2 ihre; 3 seiner; 4 ihrer; 5 meine; 6 ihre.

Exercise 5.4

1 Das Buch war interessant, aber es war zu lang. 2 Kennen Sie den Film? Ich kenne ihn nicht. 3 Das Geschenk ist für ihn. 4 Er schenkt ihr einen Ferrari. 5 Die Flasche Champagner ist von uns. 6 Sehen Sie die blaue Jacke? – Meinen Sie diese/die da? 7 Man tut das nicht. 8 Man sagt, dass Wien romantisch ist. 9 Alle haben gelacht. 10 Viele kamen zur Party.

Checklist

1 A pronoun 'stands in' for a noun and refers to persons, things or ideas. 2 Because a pronoun has to agree in gender, number and case with the noun it replaces. 4 Accusative – **mich**, **dich**, **Sie**, **ihn**, **sie**, **es**, **uns**, **euch**, **Sie**, **sie**; dative – **mir**, **dir**, **Ihnen**, **ihm**, **ihr**, **ihm**, **uns**, **euch**, **Ihnen**, **ihnen**. 5. Here are all forms of **dieser**:

	Masculine	*Feminine*	*Neuter*	*Plural*
Nom.	dies*er*	dies*e*	dies*es*	dies*e*
Acc.	dies*en*	dies*e*	dies*es*	dies*e*
Dat.	dies*em*	dies*er*	dies*em*	dies*en*
Gen.	dies*es*	dies*er*	dies*es*	dies*er*

UNIT 6: Reflexive verbs

Exercise 6.1

Reflexive pronoun in the accusative	*Reflexive pronoun in the dative*
sich amüsieren; sich bedanken; sich beeilen; sich erholen; sich entschließen; sich erkälten; sich verlieben; sich verspäten; sich verabschieden; sich verletzen	sich überlegen; sich vornehmen

Exercise 6.2

1 sich; 2 dich; 3 mich; 4 uns; 5 dir; 6 dir; 7 mich.

Exercise 6.3

1 Sie ärgert sich über ihren Bruder. 2 Wir können uns damit schaden. 3 Gestern hat sich Marco verliebt. 4 Er hat sich wegen der Panne verspätet. 5 Vor ihren Eltern benehmen sie sich gut. 6 Überlegt euch das noch mal!

Exercise 6.4

1 Ich möchte mich entschuldigen. 2 Wir wollen uns für das Geschenk bedanken. 3 Interessierst du dich/Interessieren Sie sich/Interessiert ihr euch für Sport? 4 Hast du dich/Haben Sie sich/Habt ihr euch verletzt? 5 Ich putze mir sehr oft die Zähne. 6 Ich ziehe mir die Schuhe an. 7 Wir sollten uns diese Frage stellen. 8 Stell dir/Stellen Sie sich/Stellt euch das vor!

Checklist

1 A 'true' reflexive verb can only be used reflexively. It cannot be used without a reflexive pronoun. 2 mich, dich, sich (Sie), sich (er, sie, es), uns, euch, sich (Sie), sich (sie). 3 mich → mir, dich → dir. 4 The reflexive pronoun usually comes after the finite verb.

UNIT 7: Modal verbs

Exercise 7.1

1 dürfen; 2 kann; 3 muss; 4 mag; 5 will; 6 darfst; 7 müsst; 8 könnt.

Exercise 7.2

1 durften, 2 konnte, 3 musste, 4 mochte, 5 wollte, 6 durftest, 7 musstet, 8 konntet.

Exercise 7.3

1 Der Sänger hat nicht rauchen dürfen. 2 Ich habe mehr Sport treiben wollen. 3 Sie haben in der Nacht arbeiten müssen. 4 Er hat Al Pacino interviewen dürfen. 5 Wir haben nach Miami fliegen können.

Exercise 7.4

1 Sie mag klassische Musik. 2 Sollen wir mit dem Auto fahren? 3 Du darfst/Sie dürfen/Ihr dürft hier parken. 4 Er soll mehr Obst essen. 5 Die Kinder dürfen nicht fernsehen. 6 Sie durfte nicht ins Kino (gehen).

7 Sie mussten nach Hause (gehen). 8 Das darfst du/Das dürfen Sie/
Das dürft ihr nicht! 9 Die Band wird nicht spielen können. 10 Wir werden
ein neues Radio kaufen müssen. 11 Kannst du/Können Sie/Könnt ihr
Italienisch (sprechen)? 12 Was soll das?

Checklist

1 dürfen, können, mögen, müssen, sollen, wollen. 2 ich darf nicht ... 3
dürfen, können, mögen and **müssen** change their stem by dropping the
umlaut and using the '**te**' endings. 4 Here are some possible examples:
**Ich kann nicht mehr. Wir müssen jetzt nach Hause. Wir wollen ins
Kino/Theater etc. Er kann das sehr gut. Das darfst du nicht. Können Sie
Italienisch/Französisch etc.? Was soll das?**

UNIT 8: Verbs with separable and inseparable prefixes

Exercise 8.1

1 abfahren (*sep.*) 'to depart by vehicle'; 2 anfangen (*sep.*) 'to start'; 3
aufschreiben (sep.) 'to write down'; 4 aufhören (*sep.*) 'to stop'; 5 ausgehen
(*sep.*) 'to go out'; 6 berichten (*insep.*) 'to report'; 7 bezahlen (*insep.*) 'to
pay (for)'; 8 einladen (*sep.*) 'to invite'; 9 entstehen (insep.) 'to come into
being'; 10 entwerfen (*insep.*) 'to design'; 11 erlauben (*insep.*) 'to allow';
12 erfinden (*insep.*) 'to invent'; 13 festmachen (*sep.*) 'to fasten'; 14 gehören
(*insep.*) 'to belong'; 15 gewinnen (*insep.*) 'to win'; 16 hinfallen (*sep.*) 'to
fall (over)'; 17 mitmachen (*sep.*) 'to join in'; 18 mitgehen (*sep.*) 'to go with
somebody'; 19 stattfinden (*sep.*) 'to take place' ; 20 übernachten (*insep.*)
'to stay overnight'; 21 umarmen (*insep.*) 'to embrace'; 22 umtauschen (*sep.*)
'to exchange'; 23 verlieren (*insep.*) 'to lose'; 24 vorstellen (*sep.*) 'to introduce'; 25 wegfahren (*sep.*) 'to go away by vehicle'; 26 wiedersehen (*sep.*)
'to see again' 27 wiederholen (insep.) 'to repeat'; 28 zumachen (*sep.*) 'to
shut'.

Exercise 8.2

1 aus; 2 an; 3 wieder; 4 vor; 5 fest; 6 auf; 7 unter; 8 um.

Exercise 8.3

1 ..., dass sie jedes Wochenende ausgehen. 2 ..., dass das Konzert um
8 Uhr anfängt. 3 ..., dass ich ihn bald wiedersehe. 4 ..., dass sich Tanja
und Leo auf die Englischprüfung vorbereiten. 5 ..., dass der Polizist die
Verbrecher festnimmt. 6 ..., dass ich mit dem Rauchen aufhöre. 7 ...,
dass das Boot niemals untergeht. 8 ..., dass der Politiker die Rede noch
einmal umschreibt.

Exercise 8.4

1 Ich gehe oft aus. 2 Sie ruft ihre Schwester in Deutschland an. 3 Er unter-richtet Mathematik. 4 Wir besuchen unsere Eltern jeden Monat. 5 Max muss sich auf das Meeting vorbereiten. 6 Mach/Machen Sie die Tür auf! 7 Die Milch kocht über. 8 Ich übernachte im Hilton. 9 Sie wiederholen das Wort dreimal. 10 Ich denke, dass der Film um 8 Uhr anfängt.

Checklist

1 separable, inseparable and variable (either separable or inseparable) prefixes. 2 **be-**, **emp-**, **ent-**, **er-**, **ge-**, **miss-**, **ver-**, **zer-**. 3 There is one main difference: separable verbs normally insert **-ge-** between the prefix and the main part of the verb; whereas inseparable verbs do not. 4 By looking for the word 'sep' next to the verb in the dictionary. Also by observing where the stress lies: with separable verbs, the stress usually falls on the prefix; inseparable verbs accentuate the main part of the verb.

UNIT 9: Verbs and prepositions

Exercise 9.1

1 träumen von + *dative* – 'to dream of'; 2 aufhören mit + *dative* – 'to stop doing something'; 3 sich beschäftigen mit + *dative* – 'to occupy oneself with'; 4 sich beschweren über + *accusative* – 'to complain about'; 5 sich bewerben bei + *dative* – 'to apply to'/sich bewerben um + *accusative* – 'to apply for'; 6 denken an + *accusative* – 'to think of'; 7 sich erinnern an + *accusative* – 'to remember'; 8 sich entschuldigen bei + *dative* – 'to apologise to'/sich entschuldigen für + *accusative* – 'to apologise for'; 9 sich freuen auf + *accusative* – 'to look forward to'/sich freuen über + *accusative* – 'to be pleased about'; 10 glauben an + *accusative* – 'to believe in'; 11 sich handeln um + *accusative* – 'to be about'; 12 sich interessieren für + *accusative* – 'to be interested in'; 13 nachdenken über + *accusative* – 'to think about'/'to reflect on'; 14 teilnehmen an + dative – 'to take part in'; 15 telefonieren mit + *dative* – 'to talk on the phone to'; 16 sich verabschieden von + *dative* – 'to take one's leave from'; 17 vergleichen mit + *dative* – 'to compare to'; 18 sich verlieben in + *accusative* – 'to fall in love with'.

Exercise 9.2

1 an deine Arbeitskollegin, 2 an deinen ersten Schultag, 3 auf den Urlaub, 4 über das Geschenk, 5 mit deinem Bruder, 6 mit dem Rauchen, 7 mit deinem Chef über diese Sache, 8 bei Sony um eine Stelle.

Exercise 9.3

1 Nein, ich interessiere mich nicht dafür. 2 Nein, ich freue mich nicht darauf. 3 Nein, wir haben nicht darüber gesprochen. 4 Nein, ich habe mich nicht darum beworben. 5 Nein, ich will mich nicht dafür entschuldigen. 6 Nein, ich habe nicht daran teilgenommen.

Exercise 9.4

1 Ich warte auf den Zug. 2 Lisa entschuldigt sich bei ihrem Bruder. 3 Sie freut sich über das Wetter. 4 Er ärgert sich über den Computer. 5 Sie glauben an Gott. 6 Sprichst du mit deiner Mutter? 7 Interessieren Sie sich für Sport? 8 Wofür interessiert sie sich? 9 Das hängt davon ab. 10 Davon weiß ich nichts.

Checklist

1 What case the preposition requires as it affects the endings of determiners and sometimes of nouns which follow the preposition. 2 **sich freuen** can appear with the prepositions **auf** or **über**. 3 When the object of the question is a person: preposition + appropriate case form of **wer**, followed by the rest of question. In connection with things, ideas etc.: **wo(r)** + preposition, followed by the rest of the question.

UNIT 10: The present tense

Exercise 10.1

1 fahren ✓	7 gefallen ✓	13 essen ✓	20 sprechen ✓
2 bleiben ✗	8 sitzen ✗	14 schwimmen ✗	21 waschen ✓
3 sehen ✓	9 laufen ✓	15 trinken ✗	22 schlafen ✓
4 fangen ✓	10 kennen ✗	16 vergessen ✓	23 helfen ✓
5 geben ✓	11 tragen ✓	17 werden ✓	24 gehen ✗
6 bringen ✗	12 kommen ✗	19 treffen ✓	25 empfehlen ✓

Exercise 10.2

1 fahren: ich fahre, du fährst, er/sie/es fährt; 3 sehen: ich sehe, du siehst, er/sie/es sieht; 4 fangen: ich fange, du fängst, er/sie/es fängt; 5 geben: ich gebe, du gibst, er/sie/es gibt; 7 gefallen: ich gefalle, du gefällst, er/sie/es gefällt; 8 laufen: ich laufe, du läufst, er/sie/es läuft; 11 tragen: ich trage, du trägst, er/sie/es trägt; 13 essen: ich esse, du isst, er/sie/es isst; 16 vergessen: ich vergesse, du vergisst, er/sie/es vergisst; 17 werden: ich werde, du wirst, er/sie/es wird; 19 treffen: ich treffe, du triffst, er/sie/es trifft;

20 sprechen: ich spreche, du sprichst, er/sie/es spricht; 21 waschen: ich wasche, du wäscht, er/sie/es wäscht; 22 schlafen: ich schlafe, du schläfst, er/sie/es schläft; 23 helfen: ich helfe, du hilfst, er/sie/es hilft; 25 empfehlen: ich empfehle, du empfiehlst, er/sie/es empfiehlt.

Exercise 10.3

1 ich arbeite, du arbeitest, Sie arbeiten, er/sie/es arbeitet, wir arbeiten, ihr arbeitet, Sie arbeiten, sie arbeiten; 2 ich finde, du findest, Sie finden, er/sie/es findet, wir finden, ihr findet, Sie finden, sie finden; 3 ich rechne, du rechnest, Sie rechnen, er/sie/es rechnet, wir rechnen, ihr rechnet, Sie rechnen, sie rechnen; 4 ich grüße, du grüßt, Sie grüßen, er/sie/es grüßt, wir grüßen, ihr grüßt, Sie grüßen, sie grüßen; 5 ich tanze, du tanzt, Sie tanzen, er/sie/es tanzt, wir tanzen, ihr tanzt, Sie tanzen, sie tanzen; 6 ich sammle, du sammelst, Sie sammeln, er/sie/es sammelt, wir sammeln, ihr sammelt, Sie sammeln, sie sammeln; 7 ich behandle, du behandelst, Sie behandeln, er/sie/es behandelt, wir behandeln, ihr behandelt, Sie behandeln, sie behandeln; 8 ich ändere, du änderst, Sie ändern, er/sie/es ändert, wir ändern, ihr ändert, Sie ändern, sie ändern.

Exercise 10.4

1 Sie arbeitet in Bern. 2 Ja, er arbeitet heute! 3 Sie sieht einen Film. 4 Du fährst/Sie fahren/Ihr fahrt zu schnell. 5 Sie läuft langsam. 6 Er findet die Schlüssel. 7 Ich sammle alte Postkarten. 8 Tanzt du/Tanzen Sie/Tanzt ihr gern? 9 Bist du/Sind Sie/Seid ihr aus New York? 10 Du weißt/Sie wissen/Ihr wisst, wie teuer das Leben in London ist.

Checklist

1 **ich -e, du -st, Sie -en, er/sie/es -t, wir -en, ihr -t, Sie -en, sie -en**. 2 a → ä, au → äu, e → i, e → ie. 3 **haben, sein, werden** and **wissen**. 4 Verbs with the ending **-eln** drop the **-e** in the **ich** form; verbs whose stems end in **-er** only add **-n** to the singular and plural **Sie** form, to **wir** and to **sie** ('they'). 5 The future if the context makes this clear.

UNIT 11: The present perfect tense

Exercise 11.1

Regular verbs	Irregular verbs	Mixed verbs
tanzen, reservieren, stellen, passieren, machen, hören, besuchen, reisen	*schreiben*, fliegen, fahren, trinken, helfen, bleiben, sein, wachsen, kommen, verstehen	denken, rennen, bringen, wissen, kennen, nennen

Exercise 11.2

Regular verbs	Irregular verbs	Mixed verbs
tanzen – getanzt	schreiben – geschrieben	denken – gedacht
reservieren – reserviert	fliegen – geflogen	rennen – gerannt
stellen – gestellt	fahren – gefahren	bringen – gebracht
passieren – passiert	trinken – getrunken	wissen – gewusst
machen – gemacht	helfen – geholfen	kennen – gekannt
hören – gehört	bleiben – geblieben	nennen – genannt
besuchen – besucht	sein – gewesen	
reisen – gereist	wachsen – gewachsen	
	kommen – gekommen	
	verstehen – verstanden	

The nine verbs taking **sein** are: fliegen, passieren, fahren, bleiben, rennen, reisen, sein, wachsen, kommen.

Exercise 11.3

1 Früher hat sie nie die Zeitung gelesen. 2 Früher hat er nie klassische Musik gehört. 3 Früher sind wir nie mit dem Bus gefahren. 4 Früher hast du nie E-Mails geschrieben. 5 Früher sind wir nie ausgegangen. 6 Früher haben sie nie im Supermarkt eingekauft. 7 Früher ist er nie jeden Morgen gelaufen. 8 Früher sind sie nie zu Hause geblieben.

Exercise 11.4

1 Haben Sie etwas gegessen? 2 Was hat er gesagt? 3 Sie hat in Deutschland studiert. 4 Ich bin mit Air Berlin geflogen. 5 Wir sind nur drei Tage geblieben. 6 Früher haben sie nie ferngesehen. 7 Was ist passiert? 8 Marc hat seine Mutter angerufen. 9 Der Baum ist kaum gewachsen. 10 Er ist Journalist geworden.

Checklist

1 It is normally used when talking about the past; irrespective of how long ago the event occurred. 2 Regular verbs: with the prefix **ge-** + stem + **-t**; irregular verbs: **ge-** + stem + -**en**. Irregular verbs also often undergo a stem vowel change. 3 They have a combination of regular and irregular verb characteristics in their past participles forms; e.g.: **gedacht**, **gewusst** etc. 4 When a verb indicates movement from one location to another or expresses a change of state, **sein** is used in the present perfect. This also applies to **bleiben** and **passieren**. 5 They form their past participle by inserting **-ge-** between the prefix and the main part of the verb.

UNIT 12: The simple past tense

Exercise 12.1

1 ich wohnte, du wohntest, Sie wohnten, er/sie/es wohnte, wir wohnten, ihr wohntet, Sie wohnten, sie wohnten; 2 ich fragte, du fragtest, Sie fragten, er/sie/es fragte, wir fragten, ihr fragtet, Sie fragten, sie fragten; 3 ich arbeitete, du arbeitetest, Sie arbeiteten, er/sie/es arbeitete, wir arbeiteten, ihr arbeitetet, Sie arbeiteten, sie arbeiteten; 4 ich redete, du redetest, Sie redeteten, er/sie/es redete, wir redeten, ihr redetet, Sie redeten, sie redeten; 5 ich kam, du kamst, Sie kamen, er/sie/es kam, wir kamen, ihr kamt, Sie kamen, sie kamen; 6 ich schrieb, du schriebst, Sie schrieben, er/sie/es schrieb, wir schrieben, ihr schriebt, Sie schrieben, sie schrieben; 7 ich nannte, du nanntest, Sie nannten, er/sie/es nannte, wir nannten, ihr nanntet, Sie nannten, sie nannten; 8 ich ging, du gingst, Sie gingen, er/sie/es ging, wir gingen, ihr gingt, Sie gingen, sie gingen.

Exercise 12.2

1 blieb; 2 tranken; 3 flogen; 4 sang; 5 telefonierte; 6 regnete.

Exercise 12.3

2 kamen; 3 stand; 4 gab; 5 waren, gingen; 6 musste; 7 wollte; 8 hatten; 9 stießen; 10 liefen.

Exercise 12.4

1 Ich machte einen Kaffee. 2 Wir blieben bis Mitternacht. 3 Sie vergaßen seine Adresse. 4 Sie nahm ihre Tasche und fuhr in die Stadt. 5 Letzte Woche flog ich nach Wien. 6 Die Kinder liefen/rannten zur Schule. 7 Sie arbeiteten im Garten. 8 Ich las das Buch. 9 Es regnete den ganzen Tag. 10 Ich wusste nicht, dass es schon so spät war.

Checklist

1 **Präteritum** (preterite) or **Imperfekt** (imperfect). 2 **-te**, **-test**, **-ten**, **-te**, **-ten**, **-tet**, **-ten**, **-ten**. 3 Either the stem or the whole form of the irregular verb changes; the **ich** and **er/sie/es** forms do not have any endings. For details on all endings with irregular verbs see section **Irregular verbs**. 4 hatte, hattest, hatten, hatte, hatten, hattet, hatten, hatten; war, warst, waren, war, waren, wart, waren, waren; wurde, wurdest, wurden, wurde, wurden, wurdet, wurden, wurden. 5 The pattern **i – a – u**: **finden**, **fand**, **gefunden**; **trinken**, **trank**, **getrunken**.

UNIT 13: The past perfect tense

Exercise 13.1

1 hatte; 2 war; 3 waren; 4 hatte; 5 war; 6 war.

Exercise 13.2

1 hatte ... getrunken; 2 hatte ... gegessen; 3 hatte ... getragen; 4 waren ... gegangen.

Exercise 13.3

1 Nachdem ich das Mittagessen gekocht hatte, ging ich im Park spazieren. 2 Nachdem ich nach Hause gekommen war, rief ich meinen Bruder an. 3 Nachdem ich eine E-Mail geschrieben hatte, traf ich ein paar Freunde in der Kneipe. 4 Nachdem ich die Spätnachrichten im Fernsehen gesehen hatte, ging ich ins Bett.

Exercise 13.4

1 Wir hatten uns seit zehn Jahren nicht gesehen. 2 Davor hatte ich in Hamburg gelebt. 3 Davor war er Arzt gewesen. 4 Sie konnte nicht kommen, weil sie den Zug verpasst hatte. 5 Ich wusste nicht, dass du in Österreich gewesen warst. 6 Er wollte das Buch lesen, nachdem er den Film gesehen hatte. 7 Sie sprachen besser Spanisch, nachdem sie in Madrid gelebt hatten. 8 Nachdem sie das Auto gewaschen hatte, fuhr sie in die Stadt.

Checklist

1 When speaking or writing about the past to refer to an event that occurred before. 2 It is formed with the simple past form of either **haben** or **sein** + the past participle of the relevant verb. 3 The subordinating conjunction **nachdem**. 4 It can often be substituted with the present perfect tense.

UNIT 14: The future tense

Exercise 14.1

ich werde, du wirst, Sie werden, er/sie/es wird, wir werden, ihr werdet, Sie werden, sie werden.

Exercise 14.2

1 Nächste Woche werden sie ein neues Auto kaufen. 2 Im April werde ich dich besuchen. 3 Er wird sein Haus verkaufen. 4 Ihr werdet am Nachmittag einkaufen gehen. 5 Ich werde weniger fernsehen. 6 Am Wochenende werde ich arbeiten. 7 In drei Tagen werden wir in Urlaub fahren. 8 Der Zug wird bestimmt bald kommen.

Exercise 14.3

1 Nächstes Wochenende hast du deinen Kurs beendet. 2 Morgen um diese Zeit bist du schon in Berlin angekommen. 3 Er ist wohl schon wieder krank gewesen. 4 Bis nächsten Freitag haben sie unseren Brief erhalten.

Exercise 14.4

1 Ich werde dich morgen anrufen. 2 Sie wird bis sechs Uhr arbeiten. 3 Wir werden den Bus versäumen. 4 Was machst du/macht ihr/machen Sie heute Abend? 5 Wirst du/Werdet ihr/Werden Sie nächsten Sommer nach London kommen? 6 Morgen wird es regnen. 7 Es wird nicht lange dauern. 8 Er wird wahrscheinlich zu Hause sein. 9 Sie wird sicher zur Party kommen. 10 In sechs Monaten werde ich den neuen Audi abbezahlt haben.

Checklist

1 It is formed with the present tense form of **werden** + the infinitive of the relevant verb. 2 The future tense is normally used when stating intentions or emphasising a point, making predictions and expressing assumption or probability. 3 With the present tense form of **werden** + past participle of the relevant verb + the infinitive of **haben** or **sein**. 4 **ich will** means 'I want to'; **ich werde** means 'I will'/'I shall'.

UNIT 15: Adjectives and adverbs

Exercise 15.1

1 einen alten Freund (*accusative, masculine, singular*); 2 eine gute Idee (*nominative, feminine, singular*); 3 meiner neuen Kollegin (*dative, feminine, singular*); 4 seinem neuen Chef (*dative, masculine, singular*); 5 Ein heißer Tee (*nominative, masculine, singular*); 6 in einem großen Haus (*dative, neuter, singular*); 7 ein typisches Gericht (*nominative, neuter, singular*); 8 seinen alten Freunden (*dative, masculine, plural*); 9 gute Schauspielerinnen (*accusative, feminine, plural*); 10 unseren alten Kunden (*dative, masculine, plural*).

Exercise 15.2

1 den alten Freund; 2 die gute Idee; 3 der neuen Kollegin; 4 dem neuen Chef; 5 der heiße Tee; 6 in dem großen Haus; 7 das typische Gericht; 8 den alten Freunden; 9 die besseren Ideen; 10 den alten Kunden.

Exercise 15.3

1 hoch, höher, am höchsten; 2 teuer, teurer, am teuersten; 3 dunkel, dunkler, am dunkelsten; 4 viel, mehr, am meisten; 5 süß, süßer, am süßesten; 6 interessant, interessanter, am interessantesten; 7 nah, näher, am nächsten; 8 gut, besser, am besten.

Exercise 15.4

1 Die Stadt ist groß und modern. 2 Er liebt italienische Musik. 3 Deutsches Bier ist weltberühmt. 4 Sie müssen das neue Buch über Mozart lesen! 5 Sie trägt heute ihre schwarzen Schuhe. 6 Wir trinken nur teuren Wein. 7 Wie oft sprichst du mit deinen alten Freunden? 8 Sie mag die rosa Tasche. 9 München ist teurer als Hamburg. 10 Sie ist so schön wie ihre Schwester. 11 Wir haben jetzt eine größere Wohnung. 12 Der Film ist nicht besser als das Buch.

Checklist

1 An adjective normally takes an ending when it appears directly in front of a noun. 2 Adjective endings with no articles: nominative **-er**, **-e**, **-es**, **-e**; accusative **-en**, **-e**, **-es**, **-e**; dative **-em**, **-er**, **-em**, **-en**; genitive **-en**, **-er**, **-en**, **-er**. 3 All adjectives after definite articles end in **-e** or **-en**. 4 In German, an adjective used as an adverb usually does not change its form or add an ending: **Das ist *gut*. Er versteht das *gut*.** 5 In comparisons, **als** 'than' is used when expressing the idea of inequality, **so ... wie** 'as ... as' indicates equality.

UNIT 16: Prepositions

Exercise 16.1

1 *auf*; 2 um; 3 in; 4 seit; 5 zu; 6 bei; 7 gegen; 8 für; 9 an; 10 mit; 11 vor; 12 nach; 13 wegen; 14 trotz.

Exercise 16.2

Prepositions + acc.	Prepositions + dat.	Prepositions + acc. or dat.	Prepositions + gen.
um, gegen, für	**seit, zu, bei, mit, nach**	**auf, in, an, vor,**	**wegen, trotz**

Exercise 16.3

1 ins Kino (acc. – focus on movement); 2 im Kino (dat. – focus on position); 3 an der Wand (dat. – focus on position); 4 an die Wand (acc. – focus on movement); 5 auf der Brücke (dat. – focus on position); 6 auf die Brücke (acc. – focus on movement); 7 vor die Tür (acc. – focus on movement); 8 vor der Tür (dat. – focus on position).

Exercise 16.4

1 Wie komme ich zum Bahnhof? 2 Er fährt mit dem Zug nach Frankfurt. 3 Sie kommt aus England. 4 Wie oft gehen Sie in die Oper? 5 Gehst du durch den Park? 6 Er blieb den ganzen Tag im/in dem Garten. 7 Die Kneipe ist um die Ecke. 8 Ich war beim Arzt. 9 Wir leben seit September in Berlin. 10 Sie lernt seit zwei Jahren Spanisch. 11 Ich arbeite nicht gern während der Ferien/während den Ferien. 12 Trotz des schlechten Wetters/Trotz dem schlechten Wetter ist er spazieren gegangen.

Checklist

1 **bis**, **durch**, **für**, **gegen**, **ohne**, **um** require the accusative and **aus**, **außer**, **bei**, **gegenüber**, **mit**, **nach**, **seit**, **von**, **zu** require the dative. 2 The use of the present tense. 3 *Wechselpräpositionen* require either the accusative or the dative depending on the verb linked to the preposition; if the verb focuses on movement the *accusative* is used, if it focuses on position or limited movement within a location the *dative* is required. 4 Here are four: **trotz**, **während**, **wegen**, **statt**.

UNIT 17: Forming questions

Exercise 17.1

1 Ist das der billigste VW? 2 Hat Carola einen neuen Freund? 3 Fängt der Film um halb acht an? 4 Kann man auch mit dem Bus fahren? 5 Hatte Susanne davor im Ausland gelebt? 6 Wird er seinen Führerschein im Mai machen?

Exercise 17.2

1 Woher; 2 Wie; 3 Wo; 4 wie viel; 5 wann; 6 Wohin; 7 Wie lange; 8 Warum.

Exercise 17.3

1 Wer; 2 Wen; 3 wen; 4 Wem; 5 Wer; 6 wen; 7 wem; 8 wem.

Exercise 17.4

1 Sprechen Sie Russisch? 2 Hast du meinen neuen Computer gesehen? 3 Wie viel Kaffee trinkt ihr pro Tag? 4 Was für ein Hund ist das? 5 Wie viele Leute kommen zur Party? 6 Wohin geht ihr heute Abend? 7 Für wen ist das Geschenk? 8 Wem hast du den Schlüssel gegeben? 9 Wem gehört das Auto? 10 Welchen Wein möchten Sie? 11 Können Sie mir sagen, woher er kommt? 11 Weißt du, wie viel das kostet?

Checklist

1 The finite verb is the first element. 2 **w**-questions start with a question word which is usually followed by the finite verb. The second verb is placed at the end. 3 **wer** and **welcher** require the appropriate case endings. 4 It moves to the end.

UNIT 18: Conjunctions and clauses

Exercise 18.1

1 Wir fahren nicht mit dem Bus, sondern (wir) gehen zu Fuß. 2 Meine Familie lebt noch in Wien, aber ich wohne jetzt in London. 3 Sie kocht zuerst die Suppe und dann deckt sie den Tisch. 4 Ich studiere nicht mehr, sondern (ich) arbeite jetzt. 5 Die Leute wollen schlafen gehen, denn sie sind sehr müde. 6 Möchtest du jetzt nach Hause oder möchtest du noch in eine Kneipe gehen?

Exercise 18.2

1 Sie möchte Ärztin werden, obwohl sie kein Blut sehen kann. 2 Meine Mutter gab mir immer ein Glas Milch, bevor ich ins Bett ging. 3 Ich bin mir nicht sicher, ob ich morgen kommen kann. 4 Matthias ging oft ins Theater, als er in Berlin lebte. 5 Er soll weniger essen, da er zu dick ist. 6 Sie macht einen Computerkurs, damit sie ihre Berufschancen verbessert.

Exercise 18.3

1 wenn; 2 Als; 3 als; 4 Wenn; 5 Als; 6 wenn.

Exercise 18.4

1 Basel liegt nicht in Österreich, sondern in der Schweiz. 2 Die Kinder sind müde, aber sie wollen nicht ins Bett gehen. 3 Er denkt, dass Fußballspieler zu viel Geld verdienen. 4 Ich hoffe, dass es nicht regnet. 5 Als ich ein Kind war, wohnte/lebte ich in Florida. 6 Immer wenn ich diese Musik höre, will ich tanzen. 7 Wenn Sie in London sind, müssen Sie 'Fish and Chips' essen. 8 Er möchte entweder Musik oder Mathematik studieren. 9 Wir können entweder mit dem Auto oder mit dem Zug fahren. 10 Je länger Sie in Berlin leben, desto besser werden Sie Deutsch verstehen.

Checklist

1. Coordinating conjunctions connect words and main clauses and don't affect the word order in the following clause. Subordinating conjunctions link a main clause with a subordinate clause where the finite verb is sent to the end. 2 **aber**, **denn**, **oder**, **sondern** and **und**. 3 **als** refers to a single event or a longer period in the past; **wenn** refers to a repeated (regular) action or event in the past. 4 **Entweder ... oder ...**; **je mehr ... desto besser ...**.

UNIT 19: Word order and sentence structure

Exercise 19.1

1 Wir sind jeden Abend ins Café gegangen, als wir in Rom gewohnt haben. 2 Julia spielt oft mit den Kindern, obwohl sie sehr viel zu tun hat. 3 Paul darf fernsehen, nachdem er seine Hausaufgaben gemacht hat. 4 Wir konnten im Restaurant nicht rauchen, weil es verboten war. 5 Ich glaube ihm nicht, dass er fünf Kilo abgenommen hat. 6 Er hat in Berlin gearbeitet, bevor er nach London gezogen ist.

Exercise 19.2

1 Als wir in Rom gewohnt haben, sind wir jeden Abend ins Café gegangen. 2 Obwohl sie sehr viel zu tun hat, spielt Julia oft mit den Kindern. 3 Nachdem er seine Hausaufgaben gemacht hat, darf Paul fernsehen. 4 Weil es verboten war, konnten wir im Restaurant nicht rauchen. 5 Dass er fünf Kilo abgenommen hat, glaube ich ihm nicht. 6 Bevor er nach London gezogen ist, hat er in Berlin gearbeitet.

Exercise 19.3

1 Ich fahre morgen mit meiner Mutter nach Hannover. 2 Heute Nachmittag müssen wir noch schnell auf den Markt gehen. 3 Den Ring will er ihr nächste Woche geben. 4 Im Sommer werden sie alle zusammen in den Bergen wandern gehen. 5 Du bist im letzten Jahr ziemlich oft ausgegangen. 6 Stundenlang musste sie am Bahnhof auf ihren Zug warten. 7 Wir schenkten ihnen eine Flasche französischen Rotwein. 8 Er wollte es ihr nicht sagen.

Exercise 19.4

1 Geh jetzt! 2 Er geht heute Abend ins Kino. 3 Ich werde dir meine Schlüssel geben. 4 Nächste Woche wird Margret ihren Computerkurs beginnen. 5 Nach dem Essen ging Matthias spazieren. 6 Leider konnte ich Ihnen den Bericht nicht zuschicken. 7 Sie arbeitet den ganzen Morgen allein in der Küche. 8 Ich hoffe, dass wir diesen Winter nach Österreich fahren können. 9 Ich weiß nicht, warum er nach Hamburg gefahren ist. 10 Er weiß nicht, ob er seine Abschlussprüfung bestehen wird.

Checklist

1 The basic four types of sentences are: main clauses, subordinate clauses, imperative and questions. 2 The finite verb is the second element in main clauses and in the final position in subordinate clauses. 3 Many sentences start with the subject. If any other element is placed at the beginning of the sentence the subject moves from the first position directly *after* the verb. This change of word order is called subject–verb inversion. 4 They appear after the finite verb in the sequence *time, manner, place*. If one of the three is placed at the start of the sentence the other two remain in their positions.

UNIT 20: Relative clauses

Exercise 20.1

1 der; 2 die; 3 der; 4 das; 5 die, 6 die.

Exercise 20.2

2 den; 3 die; 4 der; 5 dessen; 6 deren; 7 denen; 8 was.

Exercise 20.3

Das ist Joachim Manner, . . . 1 der früher ein Wiener Sängerknabe war. 2 dessen Eltern aus Tirol kommen. 3 der auch sehr gut Klavier spielt. 4 für den ein Kollege ein Lied komponiert hat. 5 von dem es zahlreiche CDs gibt. 6 dessen Freundin auch Sängerin ist.

Exercise 20.4

1 Ich lese ein Buch, das von Heinrich Böll geschrieben wurde. 2 Ist das der Tisch, den du letzte Woche gekauft hast? 3 Dort ist mein Onkel, dem ich mein Auto geliehen habe. 4 Das ist die Frau, mit der ich arbeite. 5 Das ist Dietrich, dessen Sohn Popsänger ist. 6 Kennst du Claudia, deren Kinder in München studieren? 7 Sie möchte gern im Ausland arbeiten, was ich gut finde. 8 Alles, was er sagte, machte Sinn.

Checklist

1 Here are the forms of the relative pronoun:

	Masculine	*Feminine*	*Neuter*	*Plural*
Nom.	der	die	das	die
Acc.	den	die	das	die
Dat.	dem	der	dem	denen
Gen.	dessen	deren	dessen	deren

2 By finding out what function the relative pronoun has within the relative clause it introduces. It can also be helpful to convert the relative clause into a statement. 3 The finite verb goes to the end of the relative clause. 4 The relative pronoun **was**.

UNIT 21: Negative constructions

Exercise 21.1

1 Nein, er ist morgen nicht im Büro. 2 Nein, sie finden das keine gute Idee. 3 Nein, ich habe keine Lust ins Theater zu gehen. 4 Nein, wir werden Montag nicht arbeiten. 5 Nein, er macht keine Reise nach Italien. 6 Nein, ich habe nicht gefrühstückt. 7 Nein, wir sind gestern Abend nicht ins Konzert gegangen. 8 Nein, er spricht eigentlich nicht Chinesisch./Nein, er spricht eigentlich kein Chinesisch.

Exercise 21.2

1 keiner; 2 keine; 3 keinen; 4 keins; 5 keine; 6 keine.

Exercise 21.3

1 kein; 2 keinen; 3 keine; 4 keinen; 5 keine; 6 Kein.

Exercise 21.4

1 Sie fährt nicht nach Wien. 2. Wir haben das Haus nicht gekauft. 3 Sie kommt morgen nicht. 4 Sie gehen nie in die Kneipe. 5 Du sagst nichts. 6 Er hat nichts zu sagen. 7 Sie haben keine Kinder. 8 Sie hat keine Zeit für Hobbys. 9 Letztes Jahr hatte er einen Hund, aber jetzt hat er keinen. 10 Ich habe ein Handy für ihn, aber er möchte keins.

Checklist

1 **nicht** usually negates verbs, adjectives and nouns preceded by a definite article or a possessive; **kein** is normally used in connections with nouns preceded by an indefinite article or no article. 2 When negating a part of a sentence, **nicht** is usually placed in front of the relevant element. 3 **nie, niemals, nichts**. 4 When referring to professions, languages and activities related to sport: **Sie ist nicht/keine Ärztin**; **Er spricht nicht/kein Spanisch**; **Heinz spielt nicht/kein Rugby**.

UNIT 22: The passive voice

Exercise 22.1

1 wirst; 2 werde; 3 wird; 4 werden; 5 wird; 6 werden; 7 Werdet, 8 werden.

Exercise 22.2

1 wurdest; 2 wurde; 3 wurde; 4 wurden; 5 wurde; 6 wurden; 7 Wurdet, 8 wurden.

Exercise 22.3

1 1954 wurde die deutsche Fußballnationalmannschaft von Adidas ausgestattet. 2 Ab 1963 wurden auch Fußbälle produziert. 3 1986 wurde der Song *My Adidas* von der Band Run DMD veröffentlicht. 4 In den 80er-Jahren wurde die Firma von Käthe Dassler geleitet. 5 Anfang der 90er-Jahre wurde das Adidas-Logo von Madonna verbreitet. 6 In den

90er-Jahren wurde auch das Sortiment erweitert. 7 1997 wurde die Firma Adidas von der Salomon Gruppe aufgekauft. 8 Mehrere Fußballwelt-meisterschaften wurden von Adidas gesponsert.

Exercise 22.4

1 Der Präsident wird alle fünf Jahre gewählt. 2 Wir werden gefilmt. 3 Wirst du/Werden Sie/Werdet ihr schon bedient? 4 Weihnachten wird im Dezember gefeiert. 5 Das Meeting wurde abgesagt. 6 Der Oscar wurde von Julia Roberts gewonnen. 7 Der Song wird von Will Smith gesungen (werden). 8 Die Kirche wurde durch einen Brand zerstört.

Checklist

1 The active (voice) stresses who or what does the action; the passive puts the emphasis on the action, not the 'doer'. 2 The verb **werden**. 3 The simple past tense. 4 **Von** is used in order to indicate by whom or what the action was done.

UNIT 23: Subjunctive forms

Exercise 23.1

	machen	*kommen*	*können*	*haben*	*sein*	*werden*
ich	machte	käme	könnte	hätte	*wäre*	würde
du	*machtest*	kämest	könntest	hättest	wär(e)st	*würdest*
er/sie/es	machte	*käme*	könnte	hätte	wäre	würde
wir	machten	kämen	könnten	hätten	wären	würden
ihr	machtet	kämet	*könntet*	hättet	wäret	würdet
Sie/sie	machtet	kämen	könnten	*hätten*	wären	würden

Exercise 23.2

1 . . . nähme ich ein Aspirin. 2 . . . besorgte ich Karten. 3 . . . tränke ich weniger Bier. 4 . . . schriebe ich ihm eine E-Mail. 5 . . . ginge ich zum Friseur. 6 . . . spräche ich mit ihr. 7 . . . hörte ich mit dem Rauchen auf. 8 . . . kaufte ich einen neuen Computer. 9 . . . brächte ich ihr Blumen mit. 10 . . . triebe ich mehr Sport.

Exercise 23.3

1 . . . würde ich ein Aspirin nehmen. 2 . . . würde ich Karten besorgen. 3 . . . würde ich weniger Bier trinken. 4 . . . würde ich ihm eine E-Mail

schreiben. 5 ... würde ich zum Friseur gehen. 6 ... würde ich mit ihr sprechen. 7 ... würde ich mit dem Rauchen aufhören. 8 ... würde ich einen neuen Computer kaufen. 9 ... würde ich ihr Blumen mitbringen. 10 ... würde ich mehr Sport treiben.

Exercise 23.4

1 Ich ginge gern öfter ins Theater./Ich würde gern öfter ins Theater gehen. 2 An Ihrer Stelle trainierte ich mehr./An Ihrer Stelle würde ich mehr trainieren. 3 Dann hätte ich mehr Zeit./Dann würde ich mehr Zeit haben. 4 Wenn sie doch nur pünktlicher wäre!/Wenn sie doch nur pünktlicher sein würde. 5 An deiner Stelle tränke ich weniger Bier./An deiner Stelle würde ich weniger Bier trinken. 6 An Ihrer Stelle machte ich mir nicht so viele Sorgen./An Ihrer Stelle würde ich mir nicht so viele Sorgen machen. 7 Wenn ich im Lotto gewänne, machte ich eine Weltreise./Wenn ich im Lotto gewinnen würde, würde ich eine Weltreise machen. 8 Ich wünschte, du wärest hier.

Checklist

1 In German, *Konjunktiv II* is used in hypothetical situations in conditional sentences to add a degree of politeness and in reported speech. 2 Regular verbs in *Konjunktiv II* are formed with the stem + the following endings: **ich -te**, **du -test**, **Sie -ten**, **er/sie/es -te**, **wir -ten**, **ihr -tet**, **Sie -ten**, **sie -ten**. Irregular verbs are constructed with the verb stem in the simple past tense + the following endings: **ich -e**, **du -est**, **Sie -en**, **er/sie/es -e**, **wir -en**, **ihr -et**, **Sie -en**, **sie -en**. 3 **Wenn ich du/Sie wäre** ... ; also: **An deiner/Ihrer Stelle ...** 4 With **würden** + infinitive of the relevant verb.

UNIT 24: Indirect speech

Exercise 24.1

1 haben: er/sie/es habe, sie haben; 2 sein: er/sie/es sei, sie seien; 3 arbeiten: er/sie/es arbeite, sie arbeiten; 4 leben: er/sie/es lebe, sie leben; 5 geben: er/sie/es gebe, sie geben; 6 sehen: er/sie/es sehe, sie sehen; 7 müssen: er/sie/es müsse, sie müssen; 8 können: er/sie/es könne, sie können.

Exercise 24.2

1 Anke sagte: „Ich muss am Wochenende arbeiten." 2 Peter meinte: „Ich bin ein guter Schüler." 3 Meine Freundin sagte: „Ich kann sehr gut Ski fahren." 4 Johannes betonte: „Ich soll keinen Alkohol mehr trinken." 5 Der Manager sagte: „Ich habe keine Zeit für lange Meetings." 6 Herr und Frau Burger erwähnten: „Wir sind im August im Schwarzwald."

Exercise 24.3

2 Außerdem meinte er, der Klub habe ein gutes Angebot an Computer-spielen und auch einen Fitnessraum. 3 Er erklärte, dort sehe man viele andere türkische, aber selten deutsche Jugendliche. 4 Er sagte, dies sei eigentlich schade. 5 Außerdem erwähnte er, es sei nicht leicht für Türken hier in Berlin. 6 Er sagte, man nenne seinen Bezirk zwar oft Klein-Istanbul, aber so richtig zu Hause fühle er sich nirgendwo. 7 Er betonte, in Deutschland sei er Türke und in der Türkei sei er Deutscher.

Exercise 24.4

1 Klaus sagte, er brauche mehr Geld. 2 Sie sagte, sie lebe in Frankreich. 3 Susanna sagte, sie sei müde. 4 Angela betonte, sie müsse am Samstag arbeiten. 5 Der Manager sagte, er habe keine Zeit für Hobbys. 6 Sie betonten, sie seien sehr glücklich.

Checklist

1 In English, indirect speech is mainly signalled by a shift in tense. German, however, has a specific verb form for indirect speech, the *Konjunktiv I*. 2 Both regular and irregular verbs form the *Konjunktiv I* with the stem of the verb in the infinitive + the appropriate endings (for details see page 181). 3 When the *Konjunktiv I* form is identical with the verb used in direct speech. 4 The following constructions are possible: **dass** + indicative, the indicative, **würden** + infinitive, *Konjunktiv II*, **dass** + *Konjunktiv II*.

GLOSSARY OF GRAMMATICAL TERMS

adjectives Adjectives are words that provide more information about a noun: 'The CD is *new*'; 'It is a *fascinating* exhibition'.

adverbs Adverbs provide information about a verb: 'This works *well*'; 'He speaks *slowly*'.

articles There are two types of articles: the definite article 'the' (**der**, **die**, **das** etc.) and the indefinite article 'a'/'an' (**ein**, **eine** etc.).

auxiliary verbs These are verbs such as **haben, sein** or **werden** which are used to form tenses or the passive: **Ich *habe* eine DVD gekauft; Das Haus *wurde* 1905 gebaut**.

cases Cases signal what function a noun plays in a sentence, i.e. whether it is the subject (*nominative*), the direct object (*accusative*), the indirect object (*dative*), or if it indicates ownership (*genitive*). Cases can also be determined by prepositions and certain verbs.

clause A unit of words which contains at least a subject and a finite verb. Examples: 'I go'; 'They go to work'. See also main clause, subordinate clause, infinitive clause.

comparative The form of an adjective or adverb used to describe something that is 'more than' or 'less than' another. Examples: 'bigger than', 'smaller than'.

compound nouns These are nouns which are made up of more than one word. Combinations can be, for example, noun + noun: 'bedroom', adjective + noun: 'grandfather'.

compound tense A tense which is formed with more than one verb: 'I *have eaten*'; 'He *will have arrived* by then'.

conditional sentences They express conditions and consequences. *Konjunktiv II* is often used in conditional sentences. **Wenn ich reich wäre, müsste ich nicht arbeiten** 'If I were rich I wouldn't have to work'.

conjugation A system of changing the stem and ending of verbs which can vary when linked with personal pronouns such as **ich, du, er/sie/es** etc.

conjunctions   These words usually link clauses. Some of them connect main clauses such as **und** 'and' or **aber** 'but'. Others, like **weil** 'because' or **obwohl** 'although' introduce a subordinate clause.

declension   Declension is the variable form of a determiner, adjective, noun or pronoun according to gender, number or case.

  In German, an article such as **ein** 'a' therefore has several forms such as **einen**, **eines**, etc.

determiner   A general term to describe all words such as 'a', 'the', 'this', 'my', 'every'. They usually precede a noun.

direct object   This is a noun or pronoun at the receiving end of an action: 'The mother praises the child'. Here, the mother is the subject and the child the 'receiver' of the action, i.e. the praising. In German, the direct object is always in the accusative.

double infinitive   This a combination of two verbs appearing in the infinitive form. Usually one of them is a modal verb.

finite verb   The form of the verb whose personal ending is linked to a noun or pronoun and takes the appropriate ending: **der Junge spiel*t***, **du komm*st***.

future perfect tense   It refers to events that will be completed in the future: 'We *will have finished* the project by next Thursday'.

future tense   This tense refers to events in the future: 'Peter *will come* at eight'.

gender   Gender indicates whether a noun is *masculine*, *feminine* or *neuter*.

indefinites   They are determiners such as 'some', 'every', 'many', which do not refer to specific people or things.

indicative   A form of the verb that represents a simple statement of fact. It stands in contrast to the subjunctive.

imperative   A verb form used for instructions or commands: '*Open* the window, please!'.

imperfect tense   See **simple past tense**

indirect object   This is an object linked to the verb which expresses to whom or what the action is being done. In English, this object is often preceded by 'to': 'He wrote an e-mail *to his friend*'. In German, the indirect object is always in the dative case.

infinitive   The basic verb form without a personal ending as listed in the dictionary: '(to) write' **schreiben**.

infinitive clause   This is a clause which does not have a finite verb but ends with a construction of **zu** + infinitive.

irregular verbs   These are verbs that change their personal endings and tense forms in a different way to **regular verbs**. See also **mixed verbs**.

inseparable verbs   These verbs have a prefix such as **be-**, **ver-** or **ent-**, which cannot be separated from the main part of the verb. See also **separable verbs**.

Konjunktiv I   This subjunctive form is mainly used for reporting what someone has said: **Sie sagte, dass sie kein Geld** *habe* 'She said that she had no money'.

Konjunktiv II   The subjunctive form of a verb used to express wishes and imagined situations. **Wenn ich nur reich wäre!** 'If only I were rich!'

main clause   This clause consists of at least a subject and a verb. It can be a complete sentence on its own or linked to other clauses.

mixed verbs   Types of verbs that take on the characteristics of both **regular** and **irregular verbs**, resulting in a 'mixed' pattern of endings and forms.

modal verbs   These are the verbs (**dürfen, können, mögen, müssen, sollen, wollen**) which express such ideas as permission, ability, obligation etc.

negatives   These are words used to negate a whole sentence or elements of a sentence. The most common negatives in German are **nicht** and **kein**

noun phrases   They consist of a noun and words connected to it, such as an articles or an adjective etc.: 'The red rose . . .'.

nouns   Words which name persons, things or concepts. All nouns in German start with a capital letter.

objects   They are part of the sentence and at the receiving end of an action: 'She buys *a car*'. See also **direct object** and **indirect object**.

passive voice   In the passive, the focus is on the action, not the 'doer' of the action: 'The children are taken to school'. This stands in contrast to the active (voice): 'The father takes the children to school'. Here, the stress is on the 'doer', i.e. the father.

past participle   This is a form of the verb used to construct various tenses and the passive voice. The English past participle of 'to make' is '*made*' and of 'to see' is '*seen*'.

past perfect   This tense is used when talking about the past. It refers to an 'earlier past', i.e. to an action or event that happened before.

pluperfect   See **past perfect tense**.

plural   A term referring to the number of a noun, i.e. more than one.

possessives   These are words like 'my', 'your', 'her', which indicate relationships between persons, things or ideas: 'This was her idea'.

Präteritum   See **simple past tense**.

prefix   Prefixes such as **an-, aus-, be-, ver-** often occur with verbs: **ausgehen, besuchen** etc. See also **separable verbs** and **inseparable verbs**.

prepositions   Words providing information about location, direction, time etc. such as 'in', 'to', 'for'.

present perfect tense   A tense which refers to past events. In English, these events would often have some link with the present whereas in German, the present perfect tense is used irrespectively of how long ago events occurred.

present tense   The tense which refers to events in the present. In English, there are three forms: 'I work', I am working' and 'I do work'. In German, there is only one form: ich arbeite

pronouns   These are words such as personal pronouns which can replace nouns: 'The woman sings' → 'She sings'. There are also other pronouns like 'everybody', 'this', 'nothing'. See also **reflexive verbs**.

reflexive verbs   These verbs take a (reflexive) pronoun such as 'myself', 'himself' which refers back to the subject: 'I introduced myself'.

regular verbs   A type of verb that changes its personal endings and tense forms according to a regular pattern.

separable verbs   These verbs have a prefix such as '**an**', '**zurück**', '**mit**', which can detach itself from the verb and move to the end of the clause: **ankommen – Wir kommen um acht Uhr an**. See also **insepar-able verbs**.

simple past tense   Indicates that an action took place in the past. In English, it normally refers to actions completed in the past: 'Last year, I *went* to Austria'.

singular   A term referring to the number of a noun, i.e. one person or one thing.

stem   You get the stem of a verb by taking away **-e(n)** from the infinitive: **mach-en**. Therefore **mach** is the stem of the verb **machen**.

subject   Part of the sentence that refers to the 'doer' of what is happening: '*The mother* feeds the baby'; '*Her knowledge* impressed everybody'.

subject–verb inversion   This is the term for a change in word order that happens when a main clause starts with an element other than the subject: *Er geht* **heute Abend aus** → **Heute Abend** *geht er* **aus**.

subjunctive   A form of the verb which often expresses a wish, a possibility or an imagined situation: 'Wish you *were* here!'; 'If I *won* the lottery I'd collect vintage cars'. See also *Konjunktiv I* and *Konjunktiv II*.

subordinate clause   This clause is linked to a main clause and cannot stand on its own: 'She couldn't sleep *although she was very tired*'. In German, the finite verb of the subordinate clause has to move to the very end: **Sie konnte nicht schlafen, obwohl sie sehr müde *war***.

superlative   Form of the adjective or adverb used to describe that someone or something is 'the greatest', the most beautiful' etc.

tenses   These are forms of the verb indicating whether the action is taking place in the present, past or future.

time–manner–place rule   This relates to the order in which expressions of time, manner and place normally occur in a German sentence.

umlaut   A mark which appears in German over the letters 'a', 'o', 'u' (ä, ö, ü) and which indicates a change of sound.

verbs   Words which describe 'actions', such as 'to see', 'to work', 'to think', 'to love'.

COMMON IRREGULAR VERBS

Here is a list of the most commonly used irregular verbs.

- In the first column is the infinitive, which is the form listed in a dictionary.
- The second column gives the finite form for the first and third person singular in the present tense only for those verbs with a vowel change.
- The third column gives you the finite form for the first and third person singular of the simple past tense.
- The last column gives you the past participle form. Note that past participles which normally use **sein** in the present perfect, past perfect and future perfect tense are indicated by an asterisk.

Infinitive		Present tense – vowel change 2nd, 3rd person singular	Simple past tense	Past participle
anfangen	to start, begin	**fängst an, fängt an**	**fing an**	**angefangen**
anrufen	to call up		**rief an**	**angerufen**
aufstehen	to get up		**stand auf**	**aufgestanden***
beginnen	to begin		**begann**	**begonnen**
bieten	to offer		**bot**	**geboten**
bleiben	to start		**blieb**	**geblieben***
brechen	to break	**brichst, bricht**	**brach**	**gebrochen**
brennen	to burn		**brannte**	**gebrannt**
bringen	to bring		**brachte**	**gebracht**
denken	to think		**dachte**	**gedacht**
einladen	to invite	**lädst ein, lädt ein**	**lud ein**	**eingeladen**
empfehlen	to recommend	**empfiehlst, empfiehlt**	**empfahl**	**empfohlen**
entscheiden	to decide		**entschied**	**entschieden**

Infinitive		Present tense – vowel change 2nd, 3rd person singular	Simple past tense	Past participle
essen	to eat	isst, isst	aß	gegessen
fahren	to go (by vehicle)	fährst, fährst	fuhr	gefahren*
fallen	to fall	fällst, fällt	fiel	gefallen*
finden	to find		fand	gefunden
fliegen	to fly		flog	geflogen*
geben	to give	gibst, gibt	gab	gegeben
gehen	to go		ging	gegangen*
gefallen	to be pleasing	gefällst, gefällt	gefiel	gefallen
gelingen	to succeed		gelang	gelungen*
gelten	to be regarded	giltst, gilt	galt	gegolten
geschehen	to happen	geschiehst, geschieht	geschah	geschehen*
haben	to have	hast, hat	hatte	gehabt
halten	to hold; to stop	hältst, hält	hielt	gehalten
heißen	to be called		hieß	geheißen
helfen	to help	hilfst, hilft	half	geholfen
kennen	to know, be acquainted with		kannte	gekannt
kommen	to come		kam	gekommen*
lassen	to leave	lässt, lässt	ließ	gelassen
laufen	to run	läufst, läuft	lief	gelaufen*
leiden	to suffer		litt	gelitten
lesen	to read	liest, liest	las	gelesen
nehmen	to take	nimmst, nimmt	nahm	genommen
nennen	to name		nannte	genannt
raten	to advise; to guess	rätst, rät	riet	geraten
reißen	to tear		riss	gerissen
reiten	to ride		ritt	geritten*
rennen	to run		rannte	gerannt*
riechen	to smell		roch	gerochen
schaffen	to create		schuf	geschaffen
scheinen	to seem; to shine		schien	geschienen
schlafen	to sleep	schläfst, schläft	schlief	geschlafen
schneiden	to cut		schnitt	geschnitten
schreiben	to write		schrieb	geschrieben
schwimmen	to swim		schwamm	geschwommen*
sehen	to see	siehst, sieht	sah	gesehen

Infinitive		Present tense – vowel change 2nd, 3rd person singular	Simple past tense	Past participle
sein	to be	**bist, ist**	**war**	**gewesen***
singen	to sing		**sang**	**gesungen**
sitzen	to sit		**saß**	**gesessen**
sprechen	to speak	**sprichst, spricht**	**sprach**	**gesprochen**
springen	to jump		**sprang**	**gesprungen***
stehen	to stand		**stand**	**gestanden***
steigen	to climb; to rise		**stieg**	**gestiegen***
sterben	to die		**starb**	**gestorben***
tragen	to carry; to wear	**trägst, trägt**	**trug**	**getragen**
treiben	to do (esp. sports)		**trieb**	**getrieben**
treffen	to meet	**triffst, trifft**	**traf**	**getroffen**
treten	to step	**trittst, tritt**	**trat**	**getreten***
trinken	to drink		**trank**	**getrunken**
tun	to do		**tat**	**getan**
umsteigen	to change		**stieg um**	**umgestiegen***
verbergen	to hide	**verbirgst, verbirgt**	**verbarg**	**verborgen**
verbinden	to connect		**verband**	**verbunden**
vergessen	to forget	**vergisst, vergisst**	**vergaß**	**vergessen**
verlassen	to leave	**verlässt, verlässt**	**verließ**	**verlassen**
verlieren	to lose		**verlor**	**verloren**
vermeiden	to avoid		**vermied**	**vermieden**
verstehen	to understand		**verstand**	**verstanden**
wachsen	to grow	**wächst, wächst**	**wuchs**	**gewachsen***
waschen	to wash	**wäschst, wäscht**	**wusch**	**gewaschen**
werben	to advertise	**wirbst, wirbt**	**warb**	**geworben**
werden	to become	**wirst, wird**	**wurde**	**geworden***/ **worden***[†]
werfen	to throw	**wirfst, wirft**	**warf**	**geworfen**
wissen	to know (a fact)	**weißt, weiß**	**wusste**	**gewusst**
ziehen	to move; to pull	**zog**	**gezogen***	
zwingen	to force, compel		**zwang**	**gezwungen**

* Normally constructed with **sein** in the present perfect, past perfect and future perfect tense.
† Past participle of **werden** in passive constructions.

INDEX

Page numbers in **bold** refer to those sections in the book where the relevant grammar point is featured in detail.